A Quick Start Guide to
MOBILE MARKETING

How to create a dynamic campaign and improve your competitive advantage

Neil Richardson

KoganPage

LONDON PHILADELPHIA NEW DELHI

First published in Great Britain and the United States in 2010 by Kogan Page Limited

120 Pentonville Road
London N1 9JN
United Kingdom
www.koganpage.com

525 South 4th Street, #241
Philadelphia PA 19147
USA

4737/23 Ansari Road
Daryaganj
New Delhi 110002
India

© Neil Richardson, 2010

The right of Neil Richardson to be identified as the author of this work has been asserted by him in accordance with the Copyright, Designs and Patents Act 1988.

ISBN   978 0 7494 6098 3
E-ISBN   978 0 7494 6099 0

British Library Cataloguing-in-Publication Data

A CIP record for this book is available from the British Library.

Library of Congress Cataloging-in-Publication Data

Richardson, Neil, 1963–
   A quick start guide to mobile marketing : how to create a dynamic campaign and improve your competitive advantage / Neil Richardson. – 1st ed.
      p. cm.
   Includes bibliographical references.
   ISBN 978-0-7494-6098-3 – ISBN 978-0-7494-6099-0   1. Telemarketing.
2. Cell phone advertising.   3. Strategic planning.   4. Wireless communication systems.   I. Title.
   HF5415.1265.R53 2010
   658.8′72–dc22
                                                              2010021075

Typeset by Graphicraft Ltd, Hong Kong
Printed and bound in India by Replika Press Pvt Ltd

CONTENTS

PREFACE

First may I take this opportunity to thank you for buying this book. Having bought it you're now one of my customers, which means a lot to me. As you progress through the chapters you'll see the theme of customers being the single most important stakeholder in a marketer's professional life. If you're not a marketer you may wonder whether marketing really matters. Simply put it does – now let me explain why!

There has been a great deal of research on the subject of corporate failure, recovery and turnaround techniques over recent decades. No doubt there are many contributory factors and each scenario is unique. However, failure to deliver against objectives largely falls into three categories, namely:

- bad management;
- lack of financial control; and
- failure to market your organization effectively.

Have no doubt that many commentators see the latter as the largest issue for modern businesses. Let me make this point clearly:

*The largest threat to your company's future is likely to be
ineffective marketing.*

… poor marketing, nothing more nothing less. Many (ill-informed) people think marketing is flim flam, ephemeral or at worst deceptive. So we'll consider the role of some marketing myths in generating scepticism (in Chapter 2). We'll also consider management implications later (in Chapter 8) as this text is dedicated to helping you to improve your marketing decision making and implementation.

Throughout my career I've worked for (and with) organizations ranging from charities to SMEs to genuinely world-class companies. I've witnessed management decision making that has at times been inspired but often ill-informed. This is particularly scary as managers only have to do two things – first, make decisions and, second, implement changes based on these decisions. Hence the aim is to help you improve your decision making and implementation in relation to mobile marketing.

As Leeds Business School's Course Leader for Chartered Institute of Marketing (CIM) delivery, I've taught students of all ages, industrial experiences, organizational types and markets. The CIM students are professionals studying in their spare time and they are truly representative of the whole spectrum of organizations involved in marketing.

They've asked a diverse range of questions all of which have revolved around how their employers could improve their marketing – I've answered many of these questions in this book.

This text is aimed at practitioners who don't have the time to trawl through 1,200-page tomes. Despite being an introductory text, this book offers insights into implementation of mobile marketing techniques and strategies that are missing from many key marketing texts. I'm confident that you'll find new information that will enable you to develop your knowledge, skills and, hopefully, attitude. These are the key building blocks for developing managers. Consider the following:

Fortune favours the prepared mind. (Louis Pasteur, 1854)

and

Life can only be understood backwards, but it must be lived forwards. (Soren Kirkegaard, 1967)

We've seen companies whose successes have been based on luck (timing, serendipity, etc). Conversely we've all seen companies who've failed for the same reasons. Undoubtedly, fortune when combined with hard work is capable of delivering beyond expectations. Kirkegaard suggests the benefits of hindsight and being able to draw upon experience. First you have to gain the experience, but how do you do this with something that's emergent such as mobile phone marketing – it's the classic Catch 22 scenario.

WHY MOBILE PHONES?

Try to think of developments that have radically changed not only your life but also those of most people you know. Your choice must be something that cuts across geographical, generational, cultural, socio-economic and religious boundaries. It needs to have changed the way we live our lives and even communicate. It needs to be at times a lifesaver and at times a mere toy or fashion accessory. There aren't many contenders. To paraphrase the late, great Brian Clough: mobile phones may not be the only options but they're in the top one!! While accepting that they're not universally popular, mobile phones are as close to being all things to all people as we're going to get. On the one hand they're disposable but on the other a diamond encrusted 22-carat gold iPhone 3GST commissioned by an Australian businessman for a fee of £1.92 million.

TABLE 0.1 REACH NEW heights, aka eight steps to mobile marketing success

'REACH NEW' Heights	Steps to mobile marketing success
Reflect on	• the role of e-commerce and your company • your orientation and readiness to change • your approach to marketing
Enable change	• by recognizing and removing barriers to adoption of good marketing practices • by putting the 'e' into your Marketing Mix
Actively communicate	• by managing your message in a considered manner • using tools and techniques that help your customers • by getting your staff to 'buy-in' to promoting internal change • your brand to your customers by tailoring your communications tools to be fit for purpose
Consider your situation	• so you know your strengths and weaknesses • and be able to exploit future opportunities • to understand how those around you can help (or hinder) your progress
Harvest knowledge	• to know you're achieving what you want • to identify where you want to be
Nurture growth	• by acquiring and satisfying new customers • through developing relationships
Embrace co-ordination	• by planning your marketing campaigns • through monitoring your success in reaching your goals
Where do you stand?	• on the key issue of sustainability • when technology keeps changing

Mobile communications (aka m-comms) will become an increasingly important tool and you'll need to take steps to adapt your approach (see Table 0.1). To 'REACH NEW' heights you need to use marketing theory to support and influence your actions. It's not enough for a book to skip to the 'tricks of the trade'. You need to appreciate 'why' you're implementing changes and not simply 'how'. Remember, m-comms are only a single component in your company's expanding marketing communications mix (see Chapter 3). Undoubtedly it will increasingly be used in conjunction with other marketing communications (hereafter marcomms) activities as part of the blend you think will give you an edge.

There's a high degree of 'fit' between m-comms and the application of existing marketing theories such as the marcomms process, opportunities with social media, practicalities such as monitoring environments, using feedback (ie research for new product development), using opinion leaders and other credible sources, advertising, sales promotion, PR and direct marketing activities. Where possible I've provided sources for further investigation that are free and comprehensive. As we'll discuss later, free is becoming the norm with online sales so the notion of asking you to pay to gather information is problematic.

An aim of this book is that your company may prosper if you glean an idea that makes a difference. Running companies is rarely a matter of yes/no answers. It's not black and white; rather, it's nearly always shades of grey. This book won't change your life… but it might help a little. So, once again, thanks for the order, enjoy the book.

CHAPTER 1
REFLECT ON...

The more things change
the more things stay the same

Crises are rarely unique irrespective of what some commentators say. Mark Twain said that history doesn't repeat itself however it rhymes, which itself chimes with Kirkegaard's observation (in the Preface if you missed it!) and those of us driving companies forward, or shaping the future agents of change, need to reflect on past experiences.

The more things change...

All managers working in business over the last 10 years have seen a great deal of change, whether it's the changing marketplace, customer needs or economic conditions. Undoubtedly, technology has been central to driving much of the change forward. Technology has changed our personal lives and has infiltrated our daily activities, increasing the pace of how we live and providing us with greater choices than ever before.

The internet is only the start...

In time, those who have not embraced the new technologies will be replaced by the upcoming generations who know no difference – the i-generations. This will have enormous impacts on society and businesses. Print media still has the largest UK advertising spend, however, 2009 saw a key development: UK advertising spend online overtook that of TV to become the biggest non-print advertising sector. This is not to say that viewing figures can't go up, say due to on-demand viewing; however, TV advertisers are concerned by:

- the continued fragmentation of the market (just how many TV channels are there nowadays?);
- the use of recorders (Sky+, V+, Tivo), which enable users to skip adverts;
- increasing access to illegal streaming of, say, football matches;
- the nature of businesses becoming smaller, with 99 per cent of all UK enterprises being classed as 'small'.

Reflect on... Activity 1

Carry out a little research among staff and friends who could be typical customers. How much TV do they watch? Which channels and when? Are there differences among age groups, etc? Just get a flavour, then think of where you would advertise. How would you measure the effectiveness of the campaign?

The gap (between online and TV advertising spend) will continue to grow and it's only a matter of time before e-advertising becomes the largest advertising medium.

In the UK, research has found that young consumers spend more time online than watching TV. Also, millions of homes now have broadband access to the internet. Hence with millions of UK consumers online in the UK (and billions globally) it's easy to see the long-term potential for e-marketing.

The advance of these new technologies has brought about a revolution in marketing communications (aka marcomms) that affects your company and more importantly your customers. In our bid to secure customers (who are becoming more technologically adept and arguably more fickle) mobile phones provide:

- the ability to communicate in an interactive, stimulating two-way conversation;
- increased awareness and enlightenment in a crowded and cluttered environment;
- opportunities to create and develop electronic commerce (or e-commerce).

Electronic or e-marketing

e-marketing is the marketing side of e-commerce. It has fundamentally changed the way businesses and customers interact. It adds value above your traditional networks. How? Well it helps you to:

- adapt to the needs of your customers – strengthening existing customer relationships;
- reduce transaction costs;
- service customers outside of the traditional time/ location-based way;
- achieve your marketing objectives by using digital technologies such as electronic devices,

appliances, tools, techniques, technologies and/or systems;

● change the way goods and services are taken to market;

● attract new customers;

● reinforce brands and enhance loyalty;

● easily update changes to your customers, eg if you change your trading hours, you can get the word out quickly.

As you can see, there's more to it than simply having a website. You're more than likely already using many of the tools for successful e-marketing. You probably use your existing marcomms and data networks to communicate with your customers. From traditional communications such as TV advertising, sales promotional activity and public relations, technology has spurred us forward to use and embrace concepts such as flash mobbing, viral video seeding and of course… mobile marketing (aka m-marketing).

Reflect on… Activity 2

Carry out an audit of the tools you use to communicate internally and externally. Include simple things such as noticeboards as well as more advanced tools. Which ones work? Why? Give them a ranking in terms of usefulness versus cost.

---

m-commerce

In future, online wealth is much more likely to come from the four billion mobile users than from the one billion PC users. We'll discuss some future developments in Chapter 10. In the meantime, remember, m-commerce:

- refers to all transactions conducted over a mobile communications (aka m-comms) network;

- is increasingly a key driver for modern distribution channels (see Chapter 2);

- will continue to grow due to the combination of ever-improving digital technology and increased market penetration of 'smartphones'.

Reflect on... Activity 3

How ready are you for the inevitable changes? To what extent are you preparing adequately for the future m-commerce boom? How much of your budget is set aside to promote change? Is it enough? Find out the extent of staff awareness regarding m-comm's role in the future. Have your management bought into the need for change? If any of the answers are 'poor' what will you do about it?

FAQ: Are we talking traditional mobiles or the newer smartphones?

Both forms will grow but 'smartphone' technology is also likely to increase the significance of m-marketing with sales of web-enabled smartphones taking a bigger slice of the four billion handset market each year. Smartphones will drive the boom in m-commerce even though they're outnumbered by their ordinary counterparts. Remember, China has many more internet users than the UK, however, the UK has considerably higher online spend than China. Both scenarios present opportunities; however, the opportunities for mobile marketing will continue to grow with smartphones while ordinary mobiles will wane.

Mobile or m-marketing

The Direct Marketing Association defines mobile or m-marketing as 'the process of marketing campaigns delivered via the mobile medium' (DMA http://www.dma.org.uk/content/home.asp). They argue that m-marketing has a number of unique benefits – it is 'always on, always with you and messages are always read'. UK mobile penetration reached over 90 per cent of the population in 2009, which is truly exceptional. This is particularly so when combined with its potential for growth, which, as discussed, will ultimately outstrip traditional PC-based browsing.

Reflect on... Activity 4

Mobile's virtues in dynamically tracking responses and its speed in responding to events make it the ideal medium for direct marketers. How would your company respond to real-time information regarding purchasing patterns? Do you use direct marketing? If not, how will you interact with future customers in a direct fashion?

... the more they stay the same

There are many reasons to throw your hands in the air and go running to the hills. The Cassandras (ie the economists) are forever forecasting doom; the Luddites are forever arguing for a return to simpler times (even if simpler means pre-industrial in some cases) and the chatterati are particularly fond of berating business (and particularly marketing) as the root of all evils (more on this in Chapter 2).

And yet the challenges facing us as Agents of Change are the same as they've always been. We need to do more things right than wrong, satisfying our customers without destroying the planet (more in Chapter 9). For many organizations, the marketplace is a difficult, dynamic and highly competitive place. When looking at many successful companies it's worth noting how many of them have customer-centric types at the helm with strong financial officers providing support (Virgin and Tesco to name but two).

In Chapter 2 we'll look at some of the allegations levelled at marketing, however, first we'll look at the notion that financial control is not relevant to marketing. This nonsense has always been peddled by non-customer-centric types. If you're in marketing you need to face up to this. The nay-sayers won't listen and you may end up feeling like you're trying to push a piece of string, however, it's a worthy cause as we shall briefly discuss.

LACK OF FINANCIAL CONTROL

If your organization can identify and anticipate customer requirements, you can move to try and satisfy them. But there is the added complication that most organizations have limited resources: financial, staff, equipment, etc. Organizations that don't adapt and change with the times are often those that eventually have to fight for their very survival. Hence, companies must seek to satisfy their customers efficiently (with as little wastage as possible) and profitably!

This may be why so many accountants end up running companies, however, the accountant's perspective isn't always good for long-term growth. It's the age-old battle between the need for longer term investment against shorter term cost or asset control. The companies who are increasingly taking more market share have reaped the benefits of adopting a more marketing orientated approach. Let's be clear from the start...

'The most important "asset" for your organization is your customers.'

Reflect on... Activity 5

To what extent do your colleagues believe that? Ask them the following:

- How do we treat our customers?

- How do our customers believe we treat them?

- What does it feel like to be one of our customers?

- How do our employees believe customers should be treated?

Accountants and other non-customer-centric stakeholders must acknowledge this statement. Irrespective of whether your company is product- or service-based or indeed a charity, you must place the customer at the heart of all decision making and planning... not just marketing decisions and planning. Where customer needs drive all business decisions a marketing philosophy has been truly adopted and implemented. Companies who adopt this into their business practices are marketing orientated. Mobile phones present an opportunity for you to enter into regular, honest dialogue with your customers. Every time you receive customer feedback your organization has grown stronger (Figure 1.1).

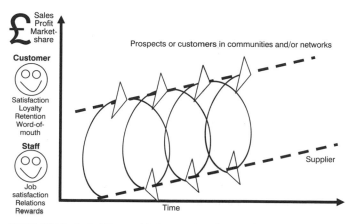

FIGURE 1.1 Flow of information in marketing orientated company and resulting benefits

BUSINESS ORIENTATIONS

Not all organizations are marketing orientated. Indeed, there are a number of different business orientations that, despite being too inwardly focused, many organizations practise (Table 1.1).

Let's briefly discuss how these could be impacted by the increasing use of m-commerce:

Production orientation – The inward focus leaves such companies susceptible to external changes (discussed in more detail in Chapter 5). As customers change buying patterns – say, using smartphones – how will such organizations know how to react?

Product orientation – Most of these adopt an inward focus at their own peril as products may be successful initially, but what if newer, more innovative and competitive products or processes (say using mobile phones to conduct new product development research) appear in

TABLE 1.1 Attributes of different orientations

Orientation	Nature	Motivation to Change	Marketing Activities	Marketing Orientated
Production	Stack 'em high, sell 'em cheap – high volume, low margin, risk, R&D and innovation	*Internal* Take share by cost leadership	*Yes* Often target late majority and laggards (see Chapter 5)	No
Product	Add to existing ideas. Some tailoring of product offer. Medium volume, occasionally high margins	*Internal* Look to improve internal or external rivals' products or services	*Yes* Target early adopters and niche markets	No

Orientation	Nature	Motivation to Change	Marketing Activities	Marketing Orientated
Sales	'We sell what we produce.' Not necessarily the first, nor the best. Can take large market share	*Internal* Look to take share from competitors by having higher awareness. Single transactions	Yes Heavy reliance on promotion – some use of mass media, others through sales teams. Strong branding	No
Marketing	'We sell what our customers want.' Often end up market leaders. Seek to innovate with products and services	*External* Seek to identify customer needs that aren't satisfied by rivals and provide solutions. Look to develop relationships	Yes Heavy reliance on market research. Promote loyalty schemes. Seek to sell benefits and add value for customers	Yes

the market? Things change quickly. When the iPhone was launched it only had 11 apps. After the first three years there were 140,000 apps. What if the initial customer response to the new product is negative? Will product orientated businesses be best positioned to respond? Arguably not.

Sales orientation – Organizations must be cautious if they use this sole approach today! The focus is on closing deals or transactions rather than developing longer term relationships. Targets are often short-term with little basis on reality or knowledge gained from customer research. Managers often produce wish lists of figures stating 'This is where we need to be' with no evidence to support the projections – often part of an ad-hoc approach to marketing planning (to be discussed in more detail in Chapter 8). The danger is that consumers can use mobiles to access social media sites for instant feedback, eg price comparison sites can be accessed in-store by scanning barcodes. You may be so busy trying to close the deal that you've missed the opportunity to respond to queries.

TOP TIPS

 By placing the customer at the heart of all planning and decision making you will be better placed to gain key advantages (see Fig 1.1).

 Put simply, if you give the customer what they want, they'll come back repeatedly to purchase your product, therefore enhancing turnover and profitability.

 Satisfied customers also tend to tell their friends, families and colleagues. Conversely, if they have a poor experience, they tend to tell even more people about it!!

ACTIVITY

 Assess whether your company has a production, product, sales or market orientation.

QUESTIONS

 What steps can you take to build a marketing philosophy into your organization's culture?

 Why is marketing everybody's responsibility throughout your organization?

 To what extent are your staff aware of this?

 What are the key benefits that your organization could attain by becoming marketing oriented?

13

CHAPTER 2
ENABLE
CHANGE

As previously discussed, companies that fail often do so due to their poor marketing. And yet there is much cynicism towards marketing. Hence this chapter addresses some of the myths relating to marketing and how m-marketing can help your organization.

WHAT IS MARKETING TO YOU?

Take a moment to reflect on how you perceive marketing – are you sceptical? Positive? Or largely indifferent? Many people think marketing is 'just advertising… isn't it?' or 'just about giving stuff away'. These aren't unusual reactions as promotional work is often the most visible part of a marketing team's effort. The notion that marketing merely churns out products, free gifts and advertising is a myth that requires dispelling. Worryingly, these narrow perceptions are often held by fellow professionals who should really know better.

Journalists in esteemed publications such as *The Times* are often sniffy about 'Marketing' while ignoring the benefits they themselves reap from their employer's huge e-marketing efforts. News International's use of m-commerce among other digital marketing techniques generates increased sales, advertising revenue and, in these difficult times for the print media, job security. I often recommend their mobile site (http://timesmobile.mobi/) to students as it's an excellent illustration of m-commerce with links to drive purchases, blogs, comparison websites, tweets for mobile users, etc.

Scepticism

There are people who question whether m-commerce can add value for companies. They argue that:

- there's no value to tweets (posts on Twitter);
- social networking sites distract employees who should be otherwise engaged;
- user-generated content is flawed as most users by definition aren't experts.

These misconceptions have some basis in truth. Tweets are essentially ephemeral (ie here today and gone tomorrow) but value isn't derived from the longevity of tweets themselves, rather it comes from how you use them. As a source of real-time research they're changing the way companies carry out research (discussed in more detail in Chapter 6).

Regarding the relevance of user-generated material, research by Pear Analytics suggested that almost 50 per cent of tweets are mindless babble – that means that over half of it isn't. It's safe to say that the internet would be a much more useful tool if only half of it was babble. Indeed, key consumer insights are often derived from 'soft' comments rather than 'hard' statistics. And as far as experts are concerned, very few economists were predicting the economic hardships prior to the credit crunch and none were predicting developments such as the collapse of Lehman Brothers.

That said, when respected figures such as Professor Malcolm McDonald say that UK marketing has gone backwards over the last decade, we need to sit up and listen. We need, more than ever before, to adopt good marketing practices and we need to better understand barriers to the adoption of such practices. Partially this may be due to the Magnificent 7 Marketing Myths that are often trotted out, such as:

1 A satisfied customer is a loyal customer

Managers often confuse satisfaction with loyalty. In some cases loyalty is simply down to customer apathy as the perceived benefits of changing supplier don't outweigh the hassle of moving. This is often the case with retail banking and utilities such as gas suppliers. We need to ask:

Has being good at systems, eg Customer Relationship Management (CRM), replaced identifying our customers thoughts, feelings and concerns?

Professor Michael Baker hit the nail on the head when he argued that instead of promoting CRM (Customer Relationship Management) we should be advocating CSM (Customer Satisfaction Management). It's fair to say that satisfied, loyal customers are more likely to provide good Word of Mouth (WoM), stimulating and bringing new customers to your company.

2 A strong brand is invincible

Strong brands are far from invincible, as has been proven time and time again. Microsoft are undoubtedly one of the world's strongest brands and yet they're under attack from all sides. On one front it's the advance of open source software (eg Linux, Mozilla, Google's Chrome) and shareware. Another, are technological changes such as cloud computing, eg word processing or the challenges presented by the 4G generation of mobiles – the Google phone based on Android. They've recognized this threat and have the financial strength to diversify into hardware. The Xbox 360 cost $3 billion to develop but won't recoup its research and development costs. They see it as a future hub for home communications.

3 A big-name brand can sustain a higher price

Dell must be the most well-known computing brand and yet they offer a value-for-money proposition. Also, McDonalds must be one of the world's most easily recognized brands and yet their prices are by no means at the top end of the scale. It comes down to whether or not the customer perceives the goods or service to be worth it. Remember it's not about being the cheapest, as many iPhone owners think their phone is the best value for money available.

4 The customer is king or queen!

The customer should be king or queen but we all know this is far from the truth with many organizations. Let me be clear:

The most important 'assets' for your organization are your customers and you must place them at the heart of all the decision making and planning (not just the marketing) decisions.

Customer needs must drive all the business decisions and this can only be achieved by entering into regular, honest dialogue with your customers. Every time you receive customer feedback your organization has grown stronger. Put quite simply, if you continually give the customer what they want, the chances are that they will come back, time and time again to purchase your product or services, therefore enhancing sales, turnover and profitability as well as striving to achieve customer satisfaction and loyalty.

5 Members of distribution channels do not influence marketing

Distribution channels are often key to the success of your company. At best poor distribution can be an irritant to your customers; however, at worst it can bring your company down.

6 Advertising always affects sales

This is far from true… unless we recognize that some advertising campaigns have actually driven customers away! Good advertising can have a long-term effect. Not all advertising is good! Mobile advertising is gaining ground as it has the unique ability to be seen by the handset owner. This and other technological changes are causing havoc in the advertising industry.

7 Marketing is only used by large organizations

If anything a marketing orientation is more important for small-to-medium sized enterprises (SMEs) to engage in than that of a global or multinational player. SMEs don't have the low cost base or the huge pool of investment funds of large businesses. Where they often have the advantage, is in their ability to move much closer to the customer, to form strong alliances with them, make them feel important and have the ability to adapt, quickly responding to changing customer needs and market dynamics.

Having dispelled the seven myths, it's a good point to look at the marketing tools from a mobile marketing perspective. To do this we'll look at the extended marketing mix.

THE E-MIX

The aim of this section isn't to introduce you to the fundamentals of marketing *per se*. For that you'd be better reading *Develop Your Marketing Skills* (Gosnay, R and Richardson, N, Kogan Page). Rather, this section should give you a better understanding of how marketing practices need to change in line with m-commerce. I prefer to use customer-centric terms for the mix, however, for the sake of continuity I've included the traditional names in brackets.

Customer benefits (aka product)

Always remember that customers gain value from the benefits your products offer. A common mistake is to simply list features in sales literature. It's not enough – you must tell your customers how you can help them! The starting point for understanding how products help solve customer problems is to reflect on two key factors, namely:

- Tangible factors – can be seen and/or touched, such as its physical features.

- Intangible factors – the power and strength of the brand, quality of the materials, customer care, etc. You can't see or touch these, nevertheless they enhance the 'product offering'.

It's important that the tangible and intangible components complement each other in terms of price and quality.

Identifying these factors can be difficult because the emphasis we place on them differs from product to product.

CASE STUDY

A Blackberry Storm (being a strong brand) will probably have more emphasis and resources based upon maintaining the brand integrity (intangible component) than, say, an HTC equivalent. HTC manufactures phones under their own brand that run Google's Android operating system and have others that use Windows Mobile. The HTC Desire is packed with features and has been described as a clone of the Nexus One, the Android phone that Google sells. With HTC the emphasis is currently on the features of the actual product (tangible components). The first iteration of the Storm attracted new customers but was soon criticized on social media for being slow and unreliable. Usability is an intangible component of the brand. Blackberry responded strongly and quickly issued a new version; however, some customers were tied into contracts with the airtime providers and couldn't get out of their contracts. The tangible issue was addressed quickly; however, the intangible factors caused some damage to Blackberry's otherwise excellent reputation.

Anatomy of a product

As well as being aware of your product's tangible and intangible components, you need to consider which aspects may create problems. All products have different levels (Figure 2.1) and your m-comms can be used to interact with the customer accordingly on the different levels. Do you need more feedback regarding the future level? If so mobiles are perfect for gathering ideas. It's particularly useful to break products down in this way if you are new to managing products or have inherited a portfolio of products to manage.

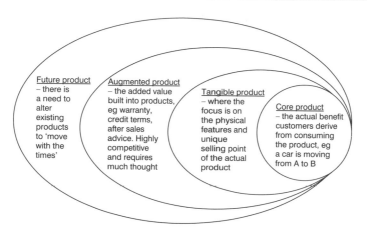

FIGURE 2.1 Anatomy of a product

The Product Life Cycle (PLC)

Products go through different stages (Figure 2.2) with some exceptions, eg Cadbury's Dairy Milk has sold in largely the same format (ie extended maturity) for over a hundred years. No doubt the long-standing nature of the brand contributed to Kraft's purchase of Cadbury. Such extended maturity is rare and is not a luxury that's provided for mobile phone manufacturers, which in turn affects those who build services on the m-commerce platform. Hence you need to understand how the life and age of a product affects your business and how external changes can affect your product in turn.

The PLC does have a number of limitations:

- It's a gross oversimplification of the real life of a product – products don't follow the generic PLC (Figure 2.2). As in the example on page 20 a first iteration may receive a lukewarm reception and you may have to rush version two to market.

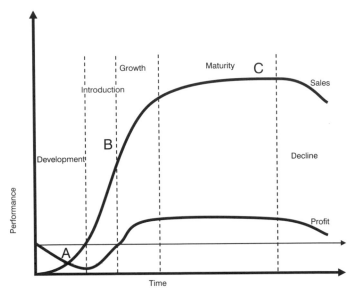

FIGURE 2.2 The generic Product Life Cycle (PLC) (See pages 104–05)

- Some products have mini life cycles due to the input of further new technology into the product to update it, such as smartphones.

- It neglects to take into consideration environmental factors such as the macro or the micro environments (see Chapter 5).

- It doesn't provide answers for key questions such as 'Do you stay in the market with this old product and maximize returns?' or 'Do you want to spend precious time, money and other resources on old products when you could be spending it on creating newer, more competitive products?'

Some marketers may try to extend the maturity stage of the product's life as their new products, for example, may not be quite ready to launch. There are a number of different strategies you can try to achieve this:

- Relaunch the product – perhaps update the product slightly with a new colour or new packaging to give it a new lease of life.

- Find new users for your product – roaming charges across the EU are (slowly) coming down, this may create opportunities for you to expand into other countries.

- Increase the usage/frequency of purchase. Smartphone manufacturers are working with systems integrators who incorporate the phone into their service. This is beyond a simple 'app', eg medical instruments are increasingly using the mobile platform thus enabling remote monitoring of conditions such as heart rate and blood pressure. This saves visits and patient stress by providing instant information. Again, relate the benefits of your products to the customers – tell them how it helps (see Activity 24 in Chapter 8).

Generally speaking, the PLCs of many products today are getting shorter due to ever-changing technology. This highlights the need for good customer relationships (see Chapter 8) based on regular, good quality communications because a disgruntled client could simply skip a generation of products. Imagine the potential impact on a supplier's cash flow!

The product adoption process

To gain entry to a market with a brand new product or indeed by updating an existing product, you need to recover

Innovators (2.5%)	Early Adopters (13.5%)	Early Majority (34%)	Late Majority (34%)	Laggards (16%)
tend to be young, professional, affluent, open minded and keen to experience new things. They're opinion leaders, influential socially and are open and aren't afraid to take a risk	are similar in profile to innovators but don't tend to have the same social standing and therefore are not as influential	slightly older than the previous two categories with less disposable income. They therefore are not as influential and do not have the social standing that the others represent	adopt products because they have generally been accepted by others. Social issues and economic circumstances play a part here	the oldest and most risk averse of the categories. Not risk takers by nature and tend to sit on the fence while others adopt products. Only buy when they feel products are solidly tried and tested

FIGURE 2.3 Product adoption or diffusion curve

your development costs and break even as quickly as possible. Therefore, there is a need to penetrate the market and raise awareness quickly and capture the customers' imaginations before the competition does. A technique that can help this is the product adoption process.

This process illustrates how products may be 'adopted'. Figure 2.3 shows different types of adopters in the market-place. By adapting your communications approach you can use them to aid how you 'diffuse' your product into the market as quickly as possible. Prior to making purchase decisions consumers often seek online materials, particularly when making larger, riskier purchases, that provide information needed to make correct decisions. Above all else, consumers turn to those who can offer impartial, credible advice. Therefore you need to design your marcomms to make it easy to reach the influencers and the buyers. Two key influencers are opinion formers and opinion leaders.

Opinion formers and leaders

An opinion former is somebody who consumers trust because of their education, profession or expertise. Using an expert can help you to build trust and credibility into your comms activities and raise your brand's profile. Opinion leaders are not necessarily experts, rather they are people consumers listen to because of their social standing, closeness or general credibility.

The product adoption process is a useful model to illustrate how consumers can be influenced by others. The different 'types' of adopters are not evenly spread through society. You could tailor your m-comms to use feedback from Innovators to influence Early Adopters who in turn influence the Early Majority. The innovators and early adopters could easily be opinion formers and you should use m-comms to seek their responses on new products. Alternatively, early adopters could be opinion leaders whose credibility could help you to diffuse your message through networks and communities. Using m-comms with opinion formers and opinion leaders can be quick and may help you establish trust more quickly than without them.

Why develop new products?

Let's be honest here! Part of the failing of the 2009 Copenhagen conference on climate change is largely due to a lack of understanding of how consumers think. The consumerism genie is out of the bottle and can't simply be put back in. Consumers aren't ready or willing to make the changes necessary to take us back to pre-industrial levels of pollution or waste or bi-products such as CO_2. Also, the needs of customers and wider society are continually changing hence new products are necessary.

If products are not simply the toys of the well off and are to percolate throughout all societies they need to be better, cheaper and greener. Technological advances will go a long way towards resolving many of our pressing issues (even global warming), however, there needs to be a shift towards replacing older, less efficient products with newer more sustainable equivalents, whether it's cars, condenser boilers or mobile phones.

Consider how the first commercially available mobile telephones looked and how much they cost. They were the size and weight of a house brick! Twenty years on and technological advances have changed the size, weight, design and use of mobile technology. If organizations still produced and churned out the same 1980s products today – they simply wouldn't survive.

The New Product Development process (aka NPD)

The development and launch of new products can create great success stories for organizations and create a real sense of achievement for those involved in its conception and development. Successful new products can:

- enhance an organization's reputation and standing in the marketplace;

- bring prominence to the brand;

- increase turnover, profit and market share;

- enhance customer satisfaction and build loyalty.

New products involve higher risk so organizations have adopted a systematic approach to reduce the number of failures, namely 'New Product Development Process' or NPD (Figure 2.4).

NPD is used to guide all personnel involved in the process – which in some organizations can range from one or two to hundreds. There are some key issues:

- You'll need to make decisions if the feedback is negative as there's no point flogging the concept if your target audience isn't on board. Go back to the drawing board or abort the process altogether. Many marketers go wrong here as they force the development to the next stage believing they're right.

- Avoid ritualistic or historical pressures, ie 'we've always done it this way' (which is the refrain of many companies that go under). If your concepts are well received, then you'll have sound data to help your decision making.

- It can be difficult stopping the process particularly when some concepts have gained momentum.

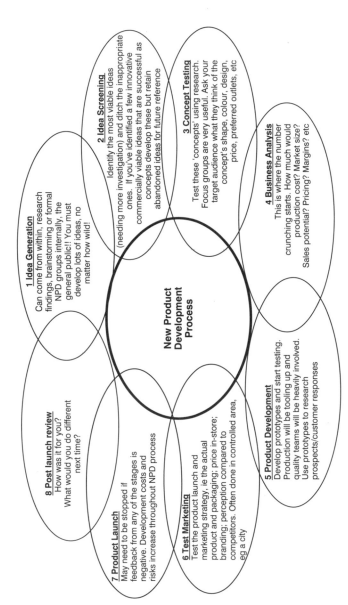

1 Idea Generation
Can come from within, research findings, brainstorming or formal NPD groups internally, the general public!! You must develop lots of ideas, no matter how wild!

2 Idea Screening
Identify the most viable ideas (needing more investigation) and ditch the inappropriate ones. If you've identified a few innovative commercially viable ideas that are successful as concepts develop these but retain abandoned ideas for future reference

3 Concept Testing
Test these 'concepts' using research. Focus groups are very useful. Ask your target audience what they think of the concept's shape, colour, design, price, preferred outlets, etc

4 Business Analysis
This is where the number crunching starts. How much would production cost? Market size? Sales potential? Pricing? Margins? etc

New Product Development Process

5 Product Development
Develop prototypes and start testing. Production will be tooling up and quality teams will be heavily involved. Use prototypes to research prospects/customer responses

6 Test Marketing
Test the product launch and marketing strategy, ie the actual product and packaging; price in-store; branding; perception compared to competitors. Often done in controlled area, eg a city

7 Product Launch
May need to be stopped if feedback from any of the stages is negative. Development costs and risks increase throughout NPD process

8 Post launch review
How was it for you? What would you do different next time?

FIGURE 2.4 New product development process

- Focus groups are particularly useful as they can actually start to touch, use and feel the product's physical prototypes. This feedback can be crucial to the successful product launch.

- What you are doing is using a test market to 'test' your entire marketing strategy. It is a safety-net situation. If feedback from the test is negative in any way this gives you time to address the problems before the full launch of your product.

- A test market situation is a great safety net device before going to full launch, the trade off is if your competitors find out where you are 'testing' they could cause problems and also have a good look at your product back at their labs.

- There is still a large amount of judgement needed… and skill. Again you may want to seek support from third parties at various points in the NPD process.

- It can take weeks, months and in some cases, years to complete and the environment, marketplace and customer are constantly evolving.

Traditional mobile phones or smartphones?

Let's be clear on this – any new products you're considering, planning or developing should be based on smartphones. They are the future and will drive growth in mobile internet services. It's only a matter of time before the only handsets available through the major retail multiples will be smartphones. Remember, both the VCR (video cassette recorder) and CRT (cathode ray tube) TV eras came to an end when the large retailers decided to stop stocking them.

As ordinary mobiles become cheaper businesses will increasingly go 'smart'. The service providers will increase their focus on smartphones whose consumers are willing to commit to increasingly longer contracts than their traditional counterparts. An alarming number of new products will fail after launch. Remember, many thousands of products are launched each year but most fail for the following reasons:

- failure to undertake the initial investment in research because it is often time-consuming, resource intensive and expensive;
- SMEs over-reliant on gut feel and current knowledge;
- poor data collection and analysis;
- inaccurate forecasting and sales projections particularly when entering new markets;
- management adopts an ad-hoc approach to marketing planning generally (see Chapter 10) and NPD specifically;
- products aren't launched... they escape complete with communication breakdown.

The advent of Web 2.0 has seen companies increasingly working together to develop new products. This has been based upon shared communications, what some have called wikinomics. Companies such as Procter & Gamble, Oracle and Cisco seek user-generated feedback on products and ideas for new products. They're increasingly using the mobile platform to enable dialogue. Cisco (UK)'s I-zone encourages employees to submit ideas and even rewards non-employees with an I-Prize for ideas. Often external perspectives can remove hurdles when internal stakeholders can't provide solutions.

Convenience for the customer (aka Place, aka Distribution)

The role and importance of 'place' has grown in significance over the years for a number of different reasons. A great deal of money is spent on getting the products to the right place at the right time. Wherever costs are high, there is always potential for savings!! If your company ships goods try to find out just how much it costs to get your products from A to B. This is particularly important if you factor products in from overseas. If you are purchasing space on container vessels, wagons or trains, whatever the mode of transport, there are inevitable costs: financial and logistical.

When it goes awry distribution can be costly in more ways than simply money. Consumers need to be kept informed (ie you must manage their expectations) and m-comms provide the ideal platform for tracking goods. If you use third-party logistics companies they may provide apps for iPhones (eg UPS) that can help you with your customers. You must make it easy for customers, so don't have complicated passwords or procedures. Make sure you can cope with periods of high demand – imagine the problems if your mobile site crashes in the run up to Christmas??

You'll appreciate how poor distribution can really affect customer satisfaction. Let's consider the impact of marketing channels on your distribution.

Marketing channels

Basically, a marketing channel is the channel through which your products reach your customers and there are a number of different ways this can be done. Therefore, channel design is important and you need to decide:

1 How long the channel is going to be.

2 Do you want to distribute your product directly to the customer or indirectly?

Direct distribution has been augmented by the use of new technologies to such an extent that a wide range of organizations now sell direct. An example of this is recording artists bypassing the retailers and shipping direct (see http://www.ukuleleorchestra.com/main/home.aspx for a good example).

These 'zero level' channels are increasingly popular as there are no other businesses involved in getting your product to the customer. The closer you are to your customer, the greater the likelihood of forming a relationship with them, receiving timely feedback and perhaps even more importantly, you will retain control over how your product reaches the customer and your entire marketing strategy.

In 'one level' channels intermediaries (ie retailers, wholesalers, agents or franchisors) move the product through the channel to the customer. They'll have an established network of outlets to reach certain sets of customers. Work with them to identify mutual m-comms opportunities and integrate each other's branding information into messages.

Convenience is also an important factor. If your organization is not primarily involved in retail – for example, if you work for a manufacturing organization – leave the retailing to the experts! Focus on what you do best. Use the existing pool of skills, knowledge and resources to the best of your ability. The longer your channel, the further removed you'll become from end users.

Accessing immediate feedback from the consumer market is not easy. Rather than forcing customers to return products to intermediaries unannounced encourage them to text you with the details. They may still return it to the retailer along with a complaint but you can inform your partner of the problem. There's a chance you can improve your communications with both parties.

If you decide to use an indirect approach to your distribution (using intermediaries) it is always useful to establish a solid relationship with the intermediaries and determine who does what. This ensures that the channel runs smoothly as conflict within the channel between intermediaries can lead to real problems.

Value for money or cost to the customer (aka Price)

Pricing is often difficult. Why? Because you have many different factors to consider and balance. Getting your pricing right is important because it:

- directly creates revenue;
- is strategically important and will be monitored closely by higher management;
- connects the customer to the supplier;
- conveys a signal about quality and exclusivity to customers and markets.

Get it right and you can have a successful product or service. Get it wrong and you may fail to recover initial developmental costs, make a profit, satisfy customers and compete effectively.

m-commerce and pricing

In creating products, costs are incurred and the first require-ment of (most) pricing decisions is to initially cover the costs. You need to know how good your offering is when com-pared to the competition. Can you charge higher prices? You need to know how much customers will pay and what their service expectations will be at this price.

Increasingly, mobiles will be used as a means of payment. International payment provider Paysafecard teamed up with BT to enable mobile users to buy online goods and services with the fee simply being charged to their mobile bill. If this payment mode is something you can use to make it easy for prospects and existing consumers you could incorporate it into your comms messages and processes.

Where there's little differentiation between products consumers are increasingly using smartphone 'apps' to make price comparisons. Google produced Red laser (a barcode scanning app that enables users to scan the net in its entirety and to access reports) while 'Shop savvy' is an application for Android phones. In scanning the whole web these sites may direct consumers to disreputable providers. As security is of increasing concern you need to ensure that your site is recognized as being secure and displays the padlock symbol. Always encourage prospects to contact your company before buying as this step will often be beyond the dodgy providers. Some sites (eg www.trustpilot.co.uk) aggregate reviews into one score.

Vouchers and cashback

Increasingly, consumers are looking to online discount and voucher providers, eg myvouchercodes.co.uk. These sites offer promotional codes often for online-only providers. The offers are often store specific, not necessarily the cheapest and usually time stamped. You need to ensure that prospects and returning customers are aware of exactly what you're offering as your competitors' prices may be lower although you're offering better value for money.

Also, consumers will complement vouchers with cashback deals from sites such as www.quidco.com and www.topcashback.co.uk who use sales to familiar online stores. The amounts clawed back vary as do the lengths before payment (in some cases it can be months). So again make sure your product offer is well represented and you don't get caught in the backwash of any cashback schemes that go awry. Make sure buyers aren't comparing apples with pears!

> Smartphone users are often involved with communities who generate a pool of advice that prospects and community members can access: www.hotukdeals.com are such a case where 'best' deals can be found supported by real-life advice that is often up-to-date and impartial. At least, they're perceived to be more impartial.

In the B2B (business to business) market, the situation is slightly different as you will tend to have a closer relationship with your customer and there are usually fewer of them. Getting the pricing correct first time is important, so use the research you've undertaken to support your decision making. However, as always, having the time, resource and skill to do this depends upon the nature of your organization, the marketplace and environment you're operating in. Pricing, although primarily used operationally to generate the revenue required, can be used tactically and strategically: to gain entry to markets and to create barriers to entry for others... so use it wisely.

CASE STUDY

The Apple iPhone (which is not only a technological marvel but a thing of beauty) was launched in the UK exclusively through O_2. The iPhone had a list price of around £240, however, it wasn't available on a pay-as-you-go basis. Customers had to enter into contracts of 18 months at up to £35 per month. O_2 aren't the manufacturers and were simply marketing a service. This service benefited from a successful launch with huge demand fed by an effective 'pull' promotional campaign. Some observers criticized the overall cost (of the phone plus contract) but you have to ask yourself what would it take for you to queue overnight to buy a product or service? It's hard to criticize customers who are so motivated to buy new products – it's so rare.

Process

Social and interactive media have diminished the power of advertising as users increasingly 'filter' their media through their networks and communities. If you need to identify and seek to change their buying behaviour, you may need to move to research via a mobile platform. This will allow you to ask questions of real people in real time, which although beneficial will demand changes to your processes.

CASE STUDY

Arguably the largest use of Web 2.0 is for search purposes and this is accelerating with mobile applications. Twitter acknowledged the importance of 'searching' when they bought Summize in 2008, which is used to search online conversations and for tapping into the collective knowledge of web users. This would involve users posting questions to be answered by fellow twitterers in an evolution of the 'Answers' model pioneered by Yahoo! and adopted by most other biography portals.

Operational aspects and systems are important but not at the expense of customer focus. For retailers, EPOS and RFID (see Glossary for definitions) are visible elements of process systems, whereas booking systems for hotels or concert venues represent behind the scenes elements. They'll all link to powerful databases, however, Michael Baker's approach of CSM is wholly preferable to simple CRM. The Co-op have developed barcode scanning applications that send the barcode to the customer's mobile (more on new developments in Chapter 10). Should the customer wish to purchase the goods they simply present the phone to the cashier. Prior to paying (by credit card) the customer is asked about the shopping experience.

Presence (aka Physical Evidence)

Traditionally the extended marketing mix uses the phrase 'physical evidence', however, it's inappropriate when considering the virtual nature of m-commerce. That said, all of the previous elements of the e-mix must help you to have a presence. One of the most obvious manifestations is in how you present your company via your website.

Web design for m-comms

Despite the hype surrounding the emergent m-marketing channel, improvements are needed before it reaches its potential. Recent developments (eg Vodaphone removing tariffs for roaming across Europe) mean that the relatively high charges for mobile internet are coming down. Despite m-commerce's substantial market growth, mobile phone users often struggle to navigate around, and make purchases from, websites.

If you want to satisfy m-customers you must ensure that your site is easy to use via the mobile platform. It's in your interest to create a '.mobi' version of your website. Give smartphone users an improved experience and make it easier for them to buy from you. Successful businesses make it easy for customers to spend their money. Hence your site will be more efficient *and* your marcomms will be more effective as users will be able to buy without the delay of waiting until they next log on to a PC. Who knows when that may be! Remember most users have their phones with them 24/7 whereas the amount of time they're sat at a PC is considerably smaller.

CASE STUDY

eBay is at the forefront of the mobile market web design and has won awards for their functional, stripped down, easy to use site. They launched their mobile site in 2006 and then developed applications for the smartphone market, such as the iPhone and the Google G1. They generated $500 million of mobile turnover in 2009 and, having been at the forefront of m-marketing, eBay should benefit as mobile browsing grows due to the substantial increase in mobile broadband.

Communications (aka Promotion)

Understanding how marcomms works, is more complex than most people realize. The title 'promotion' has been traditionally used, however, it can be misleading, hence the preferred term is 'communications' or 'marcomms'. It's fair to say that marcomms activities are increasingly becoming part and parcel of our everyday lives, therefore the next chapter will concentrate on this key part of the mix.

People

Last in this section (to be discussed in detail) but by no means least! Simply put, your people are your key assets! One of the key sources of conflict is lack of communication and 'stepping on others' toes'. So, clearly define the roles, terms and relationships early on, whether internal or external. When setting prices you may need to work with the management team to create a margin of profitability that fits with the organizational objectives. This could be based upon the individual requirement of the product; it could be that the team try to achieve a particular margin for the range; it could be a historic judgement, etc.

Training is always essential and you must pay particular attention to recruitment as training motivated staff is always easier. Armstrong (2009) suggests that employees need to be motivated to change their behaviour and that it is wrong to assume that one approach to motivation fits all. Wise words! We'll discuss how you can use m-comms with your staff in more detail in Chapters 3 and 8.

TOP TIPS

Marketing, if implemented correctly, becomes a way of doing business which must permeate throughout your company.

It's everybody's responsibility, not just colleagues who work in the marketing department. Everyone is responsible for creating the 'customer experience.'

ACTIVITY

Make sure that you view the marketing mix with a customer focus. It is most effective this way. Have a look at the following sites and see how you could use them (or learn from them) to improve your mix.

skweezer.com – Loop websites out in mobile version.
m.netvibes.com – Lets you build a personal home page from lines and news feeds.
m.brightside.com – Combines social networking and location info.
popurls.mobi – Shows who's looking at what.
mobile.qype.co.uk – Offers review goods and services across the United Kingdom.

QUESTION

Do you underpin every business decision or use of one of the mix 'tools' with the question 'How does this help our customers?'

CHAPTER 3
ACTIVELY COMMUNICATE

MARCOMMS

As technology is becoming more sophisticated so are your customers, therefore you need to understand how messages get through to your audience. To do this, first you need to consider how communication works at a fundamental level (Figure 3.1).

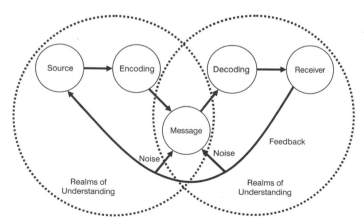

FIGURE 3.1 Linear model of communications. Based on Schramm (1955) and Shannon and Weaver (1962) both cited in Fill (2009, p 42)

Remember communication is a continual process. As your target audience (aka receivers) changes, so must your m-comms activities. Your messages need updating regularly and you must ensure you're using the best medium or media.

The medium is the means through which the message travels to the receiver. You must carefully consider the content of your marcomms activities and the media you use to convey messages. The use of a mobile platform can be extremely cost effective in terms of your sales promotional activity, advertising, etc... and in time of economic uncertainty, digital media can be advantageous.

Actively communicate... Activity 6

Carry out research to identify your target audience's (aka receiver's) lifestyle choices. If you really understand the nature and habits of your receiver you can 'encode' the messages. Encoding means dressing the message with signs, symbols and language that make it easier for them to understand your communication. Do you have focused message objectives? If you're building your m-comms around a product or service, which benefits do you need to transmit? What does your brand stand for? How much are you going to spend? This is a key factor in your media choices. How good are your competitors' m-comms? What communication tools do they use? How often? Are they successful?

Noise

When creating or sending your messages you need to be aware of 'noise'. Noise interferes with the basic communication process by distracting the receivers. We are bombarded with information via marcomms messages and we simply can't remember everything we see or are told. You need to be realistic and understand the nature of noise and create m-comms that can snake through the clutter to be the key piece of information that your receivers notice, remember and respond to.

Whenever you create a 'message' you must always be able to monitor, control and check whether the communication has worked. It's more than just a simple Return on Investment (ROI). You may spend large amounts of time and money on your comms activities so you need to know if they're effective or not. If effective... why? What can be taken from this success? If ineffective... why? Is the message unclear? Is it the media you've chosen? Is it down to noise? Is the encoding incorrect? You need to know quickly if the communication is not working so you can correct any mistakes.

When marcomms go wrong, precious time, money and resources are wasted. Also brand names and equity (the value of the brand), not to mention the reputation of the company, can be affected adversely. With marcomms activities your mistakes are there for all to see... your intended receivers, your competitors and... the press.

Social network (SN) sites provide opportunities for you to communicate on a massive scale with different audiences. Many young consumers access their sites on a daily basis, which creates a valuable means of contact for your company with an audience that is often hungry for information. Facebook also allows you to create pages that the stakeholders in your micro environment (see Chapter 5) can contribute to with a view to sharing good practice and news. While recognizing that SN sites provide access to the elusive youth audience, there's evidence that people of all walks of life use SN hence the nature and language changes on a site-by-site basis. In other words you must tailor your language to your target audience or your message will simply be lost amid the noise.

THE COMMS MIX

Web 2.0's user-generated content effectively made companies' knowledge bases and practices redundant. By 2009 YouTube saw 15 hours of content posted for every minute of the day. This isn't simple growth, it's an explosion of content that reflects many micro- and/or macro-environmental changes (to be discussed in Chapter 5) and/or changes in consumer values such as the growth in ethical or green campaigns.

Companies could no longer perceive users and customers in the same way. New opportunities emerged, eg the Apple iPhone apps market, which in turn drove new market growth. Market boundaries were redefined as companies sought to identify and target new segments. New entrants to the enlarged market had a greater freedom and were more innovative and they left many established companies behind who had not embraced the new Web 2.0 comms tools as SN sites, blogs, etc.

These tools complement the traditional ones to constitute the expanded communications or 'comms' mix (Figure 3.2).

Communication doesn't end with the extended comms mix as new technologies are breeding new comms techniques. Ironically the oldest technique (Word of Mouth) is deemed by many practitioners to be the most powerful means of communication. A new variant is Word of Mouse (WoM), which thrives in SN sites, blogs and other social media. If you are willing to pay the fee WoM can be analysed further via WOMMA (http://www.womma.org).

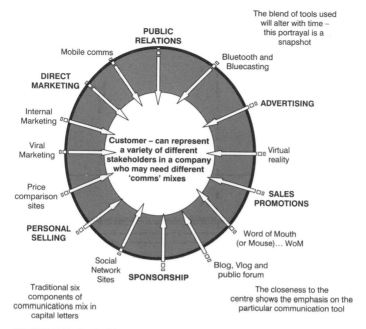

FIGURE 3.2 Expanded communications mix

WoM is assumed to be a key benefit of voice applications on the mobile platform. It's assumed to happen throughout this book and you should do everything you can to promote positive WoM.

Let's consider some of the Web 2.0 tools that fit well with m-marketing.

Applications (aka apps)

Have no doubt that apps are a way for you to connect with your target audience. Apple offers 150,000 apps and over a period of 18 months up to early 2010 iPhone and iPod owners had downloaded more than three billion apps. The enthusiasm for apps is growing and the suppliers are increasing their offerings. Apps are available in 77 countries and cover 20 categories one of which is 'business'. Apps can be designed for your company or details of your products and services can be embedded into the app. Apps provide an opportunity for you to advertise your goods and services.

Widgets

See Chapter 10.

Advertising

Apple's purchase of Quattro Wireless, a mobile advertising company, for $275 million and Google's purchase of AdMob (for $750 million) are indicators of how seriously these giants view the potential for mobile advertising. You can use ads to your advantage but they must be tailored to suit the mobile platform. A study of Kit Kat consumers found that mobile ads boosted brand awareness by up to 36 per cent. A form of advertising that has higher impact than most is 'in-skin' advertising. Effectively it wraps around a publisher's media player so the ad is visible while the users watch the material. Although more used in 'traditional' PC use it's migration to mobile platforms is inevitable.

E-mail (or more specifically m-mails)

Steve Lomax, MD of Experian CheetahMail EMEA argues that 'email marketing is rising in popularity. Over the last few years, it has proven to be an effective and measurable way to communicate with individuals and generate better marketing returns.' Recent research on mobile phone e-mail usage suggests:

- three out of four 18–24 year olds either currently read m-mails this way or intend to do so in the very near future;

- many respondents access their m-mails throughout the day, not just within normal working hours;

- the majority of smartphone users read m-mails on their mobile over the weekend.

As smartphones will routinely be used to check and respond to e-mails, particularly by the younger generations, it's clear that marketers can't afford to ignore the mobile channel. Smartphones can provide windows of opportunity for marketers and m-mail could be particularly effective at driving consumer activity at weekends. Remember AIDA (Attention, Interest, Desire and Action).

You must get the user's Attention by using attractive subject lines. The message must be of Interest to them (and not just you!). At Leeds Business School I'm constantly reminding students to make it easy for the reader not the author. Promote your brand in such a way as to create a Desire (ie sell the benefits and explain how you'll help them to solve their problems). Your message must be relevant to the user if you want to create the required Action, ie buy your goods.

There are some issues, namely:

- Contents will have to be tailored to be suitable for the smaller screens as is the case with websites. You'll have to test your message on a range of sets as they don't all display messages uniformly. Soon all smartphones will portray HTML well, but at the moment you need to be careful. You may want to consider multi-part (MIME) m-mails that include HTML (HyperText Markup Language) and text versions in a single package.

- Use shorter, snappier copy than you would on PC-based e-mails as mobile users are by definition on the move and won't necessarily have the time to drill down into your message.

- Mobile users will be more likely to massage their inbox by deleting (what they perceive to be) unwanted messages. Once the message is deleted, you've missed the boat! It's always better if you've gained the user's permission prior to sending m-mails. You must 'earn the right' to contact them (see Chapter 7).

Social Networking (SN) sites

Sites such as Facebook, YouTube and LinkedIn (a business-related network site) attract millions of users, many of whom access these sites daily. Social network sites could be the marketing channel with the most potential for your business in the short- and medium-term future.

Internal SN sites enable you to build profiles with differing degrees of privacy in your internal systems, eg intranet. Also, they generate user lists and allow access to user-generated contact lists made by others within your company.

CASE STUDY

In 2008, Dave Carroll was flying United Airlines (UA) with his band Sons of Maxwell. While waiting for take-off the baggage handlers were observed to be 'throwing guitars out there'. On landing, Carroll's guitar was found to be broken and he spent nine months seeking compensation from UA who eventually told him they were closing the incident and would not respond to any further e-mails. Carroll wrote three songs about the experience and posted them on YouTube.

The first song had one million views in the first week and went on to total more than seven million hits. During the following media frenzy UA's share value dropped $180 million over the next three weeks and although it can't be proven to be exclusively due to Dave Carroll's YouTube video, it can't have helped. UA eventually offered compensation, which Carroll declined suggesting UA donate the money to a charity of their choice. Also in a response to criticism of the UA employee Carroll leapt to her defence saying that she'd been unflappable and was simply following UA protocols. Remember it's not just your brand that can suffer – your staff can often bear the brunt of poorly designed customer policies!

Viral marketing

Following on from the previous example Dave Carroll's song not only created a media rage, it also became available for download on iTunes. Hence it could be described as one of the more successful viral marketing campaigns. Viral marketing is a potent, unpaid form of many-to-many communication that is particularly useful for SMEs, entrepreneurs, charities and other organizations with smaller marcomms budgets. Viral campaigns often seek a reaction from users, which may be simply passing the message on. Viral video seeding involves a video or series of videos going viral.

> **Actively communicate... Activity 7**
> Carry out research to identify target communities that are monitored by the traditional mass media who will distribute your viral message. Social media and particularly m-comms channels are ideally suited to viral campaigns due to their real-time nature. How would you integrate different channels in order to create links among platforms? Which platforms best suit your target market?

Blogs

Customer feedback is highly desirable and you must engage in these relationships in sincere, transparent and consistent ways. If you come across unwanted negative comments you must act quickly and professionally. Engage with the blogger, either by e-mail or by responding to their blog online. Customers will forgive isolated failings and respect companies that learn from these incidences.

> Virgin didn't react quickly enough to a disgruntled blogger whose comments on his in-flight cuisine became an overnight hit due to his witty and engaging style. It took just two days for the blog to feature in printed and online news outlets. Finally, Richard Branson responded in person to the individual, congratulating him on his blogging success and inviting him to advise on the company's in-flight menus. The key is to respond quickly, address the situation, apologize if necessary and above all prevent it becoming the lead story in the news for all the wrong reasons.

Some blogs are more important than others as they represent the views of opinion leaders, formers and mavens (experts) who now carry weight. The following are biased towards technology and are worth reviewing:

- buzzfeed.com
- engadget.com
- gizmodo.com
- techcrunch.com
- techmeme.com

Some commentators believe that Michael Arrington's TechCrunch is the most influential tech-related blog around. This is a matter of opinion, however, the quality of material suggests you should incorporate reading such blogs on a regular basis as part of your environmental scanning routine (discussed in more detail in Chapter 5). Some blogs are fluff, however, some offer the fruits of old-fashioned investigative journalism… sadly in decline elsewhere but blossoming in the blogosphere!

Actively communicate… Activity 8
Which blogs best suit your message? Does your company have a blog? Are there members of staff who would be happy to blog? Can you incorporate users into your blogs? Would your users be willing to create a community blog?

Microblogs

Twitter is the best-known microblog. It allows members to update followers with 'tweets' up to 140 characters long. These updates can be followed online but increasingly they're accessed via mobiles. SN sites such as Facebook have reacted to Twitter's real-time update approach by allowing members to update regularly with short comments or 'status updates'.

However, unlike traditional SN sites, blogs and public fora, Twitter is primarily a real-time information network. By 2010 Twitter was supporting a billion search queries per day and delivering several billion tweets per hour to users around the world. The subjects covered ranged from the bland and banal to matters of international importance. In 2009 the Iranian election was the most discussed issue on Twitter.

Twitter works at its best when the topic of discussion is constantly evolving. This lends itself well for news, celebrity chatter or short-term projects (eg Comic Relief's Kilimanjaro Climb attracted 175,000 followers), however, traditional brands with a more static digital presence may struggle to exploit Twitter fully. They should strive to improve their interactive presence as many people use Twitter to find out what's happening, not just socially but in the wider world, as the people they follow effectively become opinion leaders and formers commenting on breaking news.

Really Simple Syndication (RSS)

Many people seek to control their media consumption by filtering out unwanted 'noise' from the huge array of available media channels. They use mobiles to receive information from selected SN sites, blogs or websites by accessing the relevant RSS site. RSS sites update breaking headlines in real time, against keyword-based topic specifications, delivering relevant links to users, and relevant readers to publishers.

This makes it easy for mobile users to follow information on specific companies or sectors. RSS offers useful insights on how stories often have different takes in the global media. Sport has been a driver for many comms companies and

RSS sites allow fans to follow the ups and downs of their beloved teams as well as often providing entertaining comments from supporters.

Bluetooth

Chaffey (http://www.davechaffey.com/) defines Bluetooth as 'a standard for wireless transmission of data between devices, eg a mobile phone and a PDA'. Initially Bluetooth simply allowed the transfer of data or files between mobiles, eg you could send a virtual business card to a colleague. Recently, however, the functionality of Bluetooth has expanded into a wide range of products from hearing aids to motorcycle helmets among many others. This growth has led to increasing 'Bluejacking' where service providers send messages to mobile phones within close range or proximity. This practice is common in some parts of the world and is increasing in the UK and US. Bluejacking will continue to raise ethical questions, however, it doesn't detract from the potential for using Bluetooth as a powerful m-comms tool when permission has been granted to communicate this way.

You can buy mobile listings but it's not a good move for the following reasons

- mobile users change numbers frequently and hence any databases are quickly out-of-date;

- mobile users feel more strongly about unsolicited messages or m-spam than PC users... it's regarded as more of a personal intrusion;

- buying lists means you don't have the user's permission to contact them;

- using m-comms without permission goes against what is recognized as best (not to mention ethical) practice according to the Mobile Marketing Association (MMA) and the Direct Marketing Association (DMA).

Actively communicate... Activity 9

You are strongly advised to always seek permission from the mobile user prior to sending m-comms. How does your company monitor and react to requests to remove recipients from your marcomms activities? We'll discuss ethical m-marketing in more detail in Chapter 9.

The notion of sending codes to mobiles is well established.

CASE STUDY

Orange Wednesdays has been hugely successful, partly due to the succession of witty cinema ads and the ease of applying for the promotion. Orange customers simply text the word 'film' to the number 241 and then qualify for a BOGOF (see Glossary). The cinemas are packed out on what would be a quiet night, the users get a bargain and Orange retain a loyal customer base. On attending these events you can't help but notice that a wide range of demographics are covered. It's a win–win–win!

The Co-op retailer has experimented with sending barcodes directly to its customers who would then present the barcode (on their mobile display) to the cashier and receive a price reduction on a certain product. The logical next step is to use Bluetooth to recognize when customers are in specific Co-op stores and then send texts to offer real-time benefits.

This would be real-time mobile marketing in its best sense. The local store manager could shift inventory better while the user would pick up a good deal. It could even be used as a basis for quick real-time research, ie 'If this isn't what you want – how can we help you?' This notion of combining consumer convenience with raised perceptions of value for money is very potent. To address any accusations of promoting excessive spending, which could in turn lead to wastage, the e-vouchers could easily be BOGOL (see Glossary), which is even better as it promotes repeat visits, less waste and more chance of relationship marketing.

Bluecasting

Bluecasting is similar in principle but largely a one-way promotional tool. Chaffey (http://www.davechaffey.com/) suggests: Bluecasting involves messages being automatically pushed to a consumer's Bluetooth-enabled phone or they can pull or request audio, video or text content to be downloaded from a live advert. 'In the future ads will be able to respond to those who view them.'

Earn the right to Bluetooth

In sales parlance the notion of earning the right to ask difficult questions is well established. The DMA's version of this is a 'call to action' and where your message is sent on the basis of proximity, you'd be advised to include one. It can be as simple as having a poster at a station asking people to go to the Bluetooth zone. Without one, consumers would view your marcomms as unsolicited communications or spam. This is to be avoided! The DMA suggest four broad Bluetooth marketing applications (Table 3.1).

TABLE 3.1 Bluetooth scenarios

Bluetooth application	Example	Distance	In context or relevant	Call to action
Very close range positive consumer interaction	At shows and events and in interactive outdoor posters	A few centimetres	Yes – the consumer has to interact by offering their mobile to the Bluetooth point	Yes
Close range 'in context' Bluetooth activation interaction	The user is attending a concert and receives a ringtone download by the band they're seeing	Dozens of metres	Yes – the content is in context and directly relevant to the location/event and reflects the consumer's likely interest in the message	Yes – it's implied
Close range general Bluetooth activation interaction	A general environment in which the message is not necessarily in context, eg a shopping mall	Dozens of metres	No – consumers may regard it as an invasion of privacy and consider this the basis of a grievance	No clear call to action
Wide range general Bluetooth activation interaction	A wide area general environment where the message is not in context, eg a street or train station location	Up to 100 m and beyond if networked – possibly vast distances	No – consumers may regard it as an invasion of privacy and consider this the basis of a grievance	No call to action

TOP TIPS

 Video games can offer you opportunities for advertising and product placement. Advertising can be woven into the game and contextualized in order to avoid resistance from gamers.

 Advergames eg Pepsi's Mad Mix are designed to promote a brand or product by monopolization, billboarding and/or utilization.

 Monopolization is where the brand totally dominates a game whilst billboarding enables brands to appear in context eg roadside billboards.

 Utilization is where characters use products in an almost natural way.

ACTIVITY

 Think about the future of your company – as social media evolves it'll be less about individual marcomms channels and more about the overall landscape.

QUESTION

 What is the difference between virtual worlds, games and SN sites?

CHAPTER 4
CONSIDER YOUR SITUATION

Although I've used the word 'company', in reality there are many forms of organization and multi-stakeholder businesses; namely entrepreneurs, proprietorships, partnerships, co-operatives, charities, social enterprises, private and public limited companies.

COMPANY CULTURE AND SIZE

Each of these has differing aims and objectives. A common thread throughout these is that many make assumptions on how to make employees feel valued, often based on their own experience rather than research.

In order to communicate effectively it's important to share your vision with your staff and show how they can help you to achieve it. All members of staff have mobiles these days and you should communicate with them via this medium assuming you have their permission to do so (see Activity 7 in Chapter 3). Too many employees work in silos, concerned only with their area of expertise or discipline and lack awareness, even interest, in how the wider business functions. However, if you can help them to understand how their roles contribute to the 'bigger picture' they'll take more pride in their work, which in turn benefits your organization.

CULTURE

If you're involved in service provision and particularly online service provision, it will be reflected in your company's culture. Why online service provision over any other form of service? Well, online and particularly mobile consumers are particularly discerning and prepared to move if they're not satisfied with the service *and* how the sites work. Sometimes problems occur because of the perception of the service rather than the reality. Service quality can be measured although it's difficult and you may wish to seek outside help.

Other issues with service provision are:

- they are 'unsought' in that customers may be unaware of the need for some services;
- not all consumers can clearly articulate their needs and may become frustrated;
- services can't be tested before purchase hence there's a degree of risk;
- hyper-competition means that switching from one provider to another is easy.

You can achieve a competitive advantage by delivering consistently higher quality service than your competitors.

Consider your situation... Activity 10

Use m-marketing research (see Chapter 6) to learn more about your clients' expectations and perceptions. This also applies if you're providing services to colleagues in other departments or within the same parent organization.

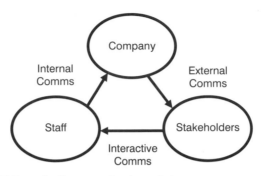

FIGURE 4.1 Communications links.
Adapted from Kotler *et al* (2005) p 635

Internal marketing communications (Figure 4.1) is essential if you're to satisfy the end-user. At times you must sell the benefits to your colleagues. Get them to see the big picture if customer service expectations are to be exceeded and not just met. To be effective internal marketing needs top management to be fully committed, which sadly isn't always the case. We'll discuss this more in Chapter 7 when considering the role of internal m-comms and building relationships.

Internal mobile-communications (or m-comms)

Employees must be viewed as ambassadors for your business and should have a real stake in making your business a success.

Consider your situation... Activity 11
Keep your staff well informed by engaging them in two-way m-comms. Allow them to feed back their views on the business. This will enhance the relationship and add value to your business.

Improving internal m-comms is beneficial for large employers and SMEs alike. It's particularly useful for companies who want to rebrand as management can have a better understanding of how stakeholders view the business, with internal stakeholders making a key contribution.

The basic requirements for good internal communications include:

1 general information about the organization;
2 specific information about their role in the organization;
3 clarity around their role;
4 a clear understanding of the organization's vision;
5 information on workplace practices;
6 opportunities to be involved and consulted;
7 feedback on performance;
8 access to training and development;
9 access to communication channels.

An internal communications strategy that addresses these needs effectively should produce an engaged workforce who enjoy their work because they feel valued.

Consider your situation… Activity 12

Use the nine indicators in the list above to carry out an audit of your internal communications. If you score nine out of nine you're a star and will no doubt be reaping the benefits. If, however, it's six or less you may want to rethink your approach to communicating with your staff. You must demonstrate a commitment to the process of gathering your staff's views of the business and issues affecting their job satisfaction. If they don't feel valued then you must address this by making a 'visible' effort to listen to them. Use text messages to identify their concerns. Allow them to be anonymous if you want to avoid bias – possibly using an outside source as the recipient.

The knowledge you gather will identify patterns and inconsistencies that you can act upon in a positive way. If you've engaged and rewarded staff for their efforts, you'll reap the benefits of having a committed and focused workforce, on message and on your side. So don't hide in the office, follow Tom Peter's advice and manage by wandering around – meet the teams that help you to make your business what it is. Give them your mobile number!

Controlling the internal message

You probably already use many of the normal tools used to communicate with internal stakeholders, eg noticeboards, meetings, intranets, events and newsletters. How do you know how effective these tools are? Does pinning a poster on a noticeboard work? Where possible provide the information where the stakeholders can access it via mobile. Producing e-newsletters on a regular basis can provide a rich source of information to staff while incurring low production costs and with a small environmental footprint. If you've scored poorly in Activity 12 you could improve your rating by issuing e-newsletters:

- featuring articles on staff achievements, both professional and personal;
- applauding outstanding performances in the workplace;

- providing regular updates from the management on business matters;

- being colourful and easy to read on the mobile platform providing links to more detailed articles on a .mobi site or via an intranet;

- signposting podcasts and/or vodcasts (downloadable audio on video media files) as (eg with YouTube) people are increasingly used to seeing video as against reading 'copy'.

Intranets are useful tools but shouldn't be relied on as the sole way to communicate with staff. It's better if your staff can rather interact with managers face to face (hence the aforementioned vodcasts) than only in newsletters – get your managers to post regular features; it helps to break down barriers.

More companies now use their own SN sites for staff and other stakeholders. These can reduce the time staff spend on personal SN sites as well as gather feedback and latest trends from staff. There have been incidences of staff abusing the use of the internet at work, which at times has provoked a draconian reaction from the company.

One wonders how much of this is due to poor internal communications, employee dissatisfaction and a lack of transparency or clear protocols by employers. It's worth questioning why your staff feel the need to 'go public'. Often it is a lack of healthy dialogue, which can be addressed to some extent with the better use of m-comms.

Using m-comms to add value for external stakeholders

The use of language is one of the key reflections of your company's culture and increasingly you'll be held to account for the activities and communications within your supply chain (see Chapter 10) as well as your staff. The great divide isn't between manager and employee, nor is it between you and your suppliers. It's between those who are customer-centric and those who are not.

Consider your situation... Activity 13

You need to ensure that everyone in your supply chain, networks and communities promotes your values and has your customers' best interests at heart. Carry out research to find out how they pass your message on to customers or other intermediaries.

How you communicate will depend on a range of issues, however, a key one is the amount of demand for your goods and services. You'll communicate with your intermediaries via a pull strategy if there's high demand or via a push strategy if demand is 'normal'. Let's discuss these in more detail.

Push and pull communications

A push strategy is where you generate messages to help 'push' your goods and services through your marketing channels from one intermediary to the next until it reaches the end user. Always remember that your customer is not always the end user and you need to be sensitive to their needs. 'Push' marketing often uses traditional 'Above the line' comms tools (see Figure 3.2), eg advertising. It can be costly, however you can measure the effects and establish a return on your marcomms investment (ROMI).

Pull strategies respond to high demand from the end users. In some cases they're used to stimulate demand by nudging prospects into buying goods. Note the terminology – marketers don't have magic wands and can't mesmerize consumers. In the vast majority of cases people ask for and purchase products and services to satisfy a need or desire that they've already recognized. With pull strategies the customer is often the end user. Pull strategies work where there is great demand for your goods or services.

Apple are past-masters at generating a buzz and often avoid launching key products at industry events such as the Consumer Electronics Show in Las Vegas (http://www.cesweb.org/). With the Apple iPhone potential buyers literally queued around the block. With the iPad Apple threatened legal actions against a US-based website who offered rewards for pictures of the product pre-launch – $50,000 was offered for a picture of Steve Job holding the iPad. Either way, potential buyers (ie prospects) of new Apple products create demand for the products and also for information, with Twitter and other SN sites awash with speculation.

m-marketing is appropriate for all shapes and sizes of companies

It fits well with the lifestyles of busy execs in large companies who need information 'on-tap', while SMEs can exploit synergies, eg easily share links, thoughts, development ideas in seconds. Existing marketing tools were developed for use with larger companies, however, the circumstances and characteristics of SMEs necessitate different approaches.

SMEs tend to adopt the characteristics of owner/managers and tend to be more intuitive. This lends itself well to social media sites such as LinkedIn. SMEs are of increasing importance economically as in the UK there are 2.5 million enterprises of which 99 per cent are SMEs. Recent estimates suggest the SME sector's annual turnover exceeds £1 trillion, which represents nearly half of the UK's private-sector economic activity. However, marketing texts have largely ignored SMEs as they predominantly focus on larger companies. This trend is now changing with increasing numbers of SMEs buying and selling goods and services online.

SMEs can form strong alliances with clients making them feel important; they have the ability to react quickly to changing customer needs and market dynamics. The financial restrictions faced by many SMEs coupled with the time demands of the owner/managers undoubtedly contribute to the lack of co-ordinated marketing. However, these barriers should not prevent the adoption of m-marketing tools such as Public Relations (PR) and networking.

PR has many benefits and few downfalls for SMEs. There is a wide range of third parties, from agencies, to consultants to your local business school. One of them will be able to help at an affordable budget. Another tool that is often undertaken intuitively is networking. Nowadays there are many events suitable for SME managers such as those run by the Chambers of Commerce. Also, don't underestimate the potential for SN sites. It's not all Facebook and Gurgle (Mothercare's SN site – great name!). Try LinkedIn, which is a business-related network site that's been operating since 2002.

Some barriers to SME adoption of e-commerce do exist such as:

- SMEs lack awareness in terms of sources of assistance, eg grants;
- they perceive IT skills problems;
- they feel their company size is too small to benefit;

- they perceive the required technology to be too expensive/complicated or incompatible with in-house systems.

The social media tools are changing at an ever-increasing rate but a constant is that customers (internal and external) need to know the benefits of what you offer them. This never changes!

CHAPTER 5
CONSIDER YOUR SITUATION (II)

As discussed, your company will benefit from adopting a marketing orientation. To be more successful, you need to be externally focused. You certainly need excellent production techniques, products and sales initiatives but the need for awareness of customer changes and other factors at play in the wider environment is paramount. Wherever you see changes in the market or environment, you must adapt, otherwise you risk being left behind.

THE NEED TO MONITOR YOUR ENVIRONMENTS

Just take a minute to think about how the world has changed over the last thirty years. Technology has accelerated the rate of change in ways that have affected our lives beyond recognition. Therefore, all organizations have to continually monitor the factors that are operating outside the organization as well as inside it, to ensure it changes with the times. These factors are known collectively in marketing terms as the 'marketing environment'.

THE MARKETING ENVIRONMENT

The marketing environment consists of factors that are:

- external and beyond the control of the organization – these factors are known collectively as the 'macro environment' or the 'situational environment';

- internal and specific to particular industries or organizations and where an organization, to a certain degree, has a certain amount of control over them – often referred to as the 'micro environment'.

Irrespective of your organizational size or type, you must monitor the forces at work externally that can impact on the customer. Environmental scanning is the term often used to describe the systems used to survey the changing environment on a regular basis.

Consider your situation (II) ... Activity 14

You or someone you appoint must take responsibility for scanning the external environments. Read quality newspapers to keep abreast of key issues, watch business-related news programmes, network with your business community via your local business school or Chamber of Commerce (they'll have access to reports and market intelligence, eg from the likes of Mintel and Datamonitor), be organized and systematic as the world of m-commerce is volatile and fast changing.

The macro environment

The macro environment is volatile, consisting of uncontrollable forces (see STEELPIES in Figure 5.1) that are constantly moving and can have a profound impact upon your communications.

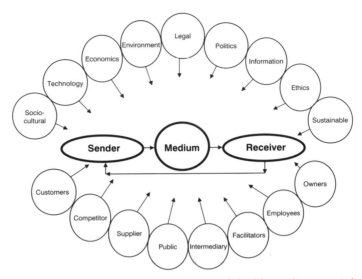

FIGURE 5.1 Communication model with environmental interaction

Remember these forces don't operate in isolation – they interact – they can constrain each other or they can energize each other. Therefore you need to take advantage of any opportunities that arise and steer your business and marcomms activities clear of any threats. All of your marcomms efforts are at the mercy of the above forces.

PEST has acted as the springboard for the most commonly used frameworks (Figure 5.2).

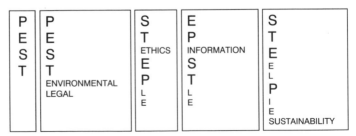

FIGURE 5.2 PEST and other macro frameworks

There are some aspects worth considering before choosing a framework:

- the CIM's (Chartered Institute of Marketing) preferred framework is PESTEL;

- some use Educational as one of the STEEPLE variants, however, this could be covered by Informational, which refers to knowledge and knowledge management;

- charities could use STEEPLE due to the ethical angle;

- new technology companies would deem Information to be key and thus use EPISTLE;

- only STEEL PIES covers all of the factors and specifies the increasingly important Sustainability.

Consider your situation (II) ... Activity 15
Identify which macro framework best suits your company and marketplace. Be clear on the differences as no one framework is better than any other.

Let's briefly consider some key 'macro' factors using the EPISTLE framework.

Economics

As the economy in the UK and USA continued to slow and fall deeper into recession in 2008–09, the downturn provided opportunities and threats to businesses and their marcomms activities. As consumer spending and confidence fell, businesses were forced to look at ways to increase their income while continuing to provide customer satisfaction in very effective and efficient ways.

Sales promotional activities both traditionally and through more contemporary digital media were used more frequently as a means to stimulate consumer behaviour and to 'add value' and 'incentivize'. However, one online SN, HopOnThis. com chose to reward its users with free goodies for doing what came naturally, namely sharing their photos, blogging and inviting friends to join them in a virtual community.

Politics

Governments have a direct impact upon your m-comms activities and intentions. In the 2009 *Digital Britain* report the government announced its intention to increase broadband speeds and accessibility of the internet to UK homes. This will provide greater opportunities to target prospects and convert them to customers.

Mobile telecoms companies, eg Vodafone, paid huge sums to acquire the licences and hence actively drove the promotion of text and MMS (multimedia messaging) technologies, which in turn increased the traffic on their networks. Some commentators thought that the sums paid for licences in the UK (£23 billion) acted as a serious brake on the development of the 3G market. The forthcoming 4G revolution presents if anything even greater opportunities for change and it's to be hoped that the politicians don't kill the golden goose.

It's the government who creates social, economic and environmental policies, therefore you need to be aware of changes. Your local Chamber of Commerce is an excellent source of information as they closely analyse the impact of legislation on the business sector.

It's not enough to simply monitor the political environment and then react to changes. Jonathon Porritt (2005) argues that:

the onus is increasingly on companies to be proactive rather than reactive, to anticipate inevitable change, to fill the space available to them for much more environmentally and socially responsible actions, and to lobby government for faster change.

Considering that 'government' covers local, national and international government it is safe to assume that your remits are becoming increasingly complex. It's not enough that you compete; you're expected to lobby as well.

Consider your situation (II) ... Activity 16
Download a copy of *Digital Britain* and identify areas of opportunity and threat for your company. How do you analyse the political changes (therein) that could affect your company? Who monitors the international, national and local government changes? How do these changes impact on your company? Post It on your website and invite your staff to comment via the mobile platform.

Information

Information provides the basis of effective decision making and therefore its availability and content accuracy is an issue. Web 2.0 has created an explosion of accessibility to information and for an increasingly wider audience. Smartphones provide access via SN sites to your own branded site and enables improved communication with users. Reading blogs and general information on SN sites provides you with an additional dimension to information. You can learn a lot from bloggers and users that allows you to encode your messages to them better than ever before, targeting potential customers with greater precision.

Socio-cultural issues

Lifestyle, hobbies and attitudes have evolved and naturally what we deem acceptable in how we communicate has changed tremendously. Increasing disposable income and leisure time have increased the ways of satisfying our needs. In the UK an ageing population and a shrinking youth market has seen businesses adapting their targeting accordingly.

A prime example of business' comms activities changing to reflect the current circumstances of society is with social networking (aka SN) sites. SN has evolved, particularly in the youth market and you must monitor these sites to be able to respond to opportunities, or threats that arise. You'll need to respond quickly as online customers and prospects can be fickle and the 'trend' of the moment can be gone very quickly.

It is difficult to predict to what extent our media consumption habits will change in the future. However we're already reading less hard copy newspapers, preferring to get our news online and our television viewing habits are changing with more viewing 'on demand' options. However, the current generation of 20-year-olds doesn't read newspapers in anything like the same numbers as previous generations.

In 10 to 20 years' time when the current youngsters are the Captains of Industry it's hard to imagine that they'll see newspapers as their first-choice communications channel. Multimedia smartphones and readers such as the iPad or Kindle will increasingly provide opportunities to access differing media, eg news, and will mitigate some current socio-environmental concerns about the destruction of trees for the production of traditional media.

Technology and m-communications

E-marketing has at times struggled to keep up with the pace of technological change. If anything, change is accelerating and you need to be aware of how new technologies can help you to achieve your corporate and marketing objectives. In 2009 MySpace became the first large SN site to become available through TV sets. Samsung, Panasonic and Sony were all marketing internet-enabled TV in 2009. Around the same time in the UK Channel 5 announced that most of its key outputs were to be shown on YouTube thus creating a virtuous circle of converging technologies with SN being Yin to TV's Yan.

These sets will eventually converge with your smartphones so you can be a genuine multi-tasker. Research showed a huge increase in people accessing SN sites or blogs via their mobile or PDA (see Glossary) on a daily basis. This growth means social media tools will become increasingly important for marcomms. The arrival of 3G handsets saw a new medium open up through the use of multimedia messaging (MMS) technology. The next generation (ie 4G) will see the smartphone become your most important device (discussed in more detail in Chapter 10).

Legal concerns

You need an appreciation of any legislation that can seriously affect your m-comms activities and also that which is pending. The UK communications industry is regulated through a combination of self-regulation and statutory requirement. In 2004 the UK saw a major shift in the regulation of marcomms when the Advertising Standards Authority (ASA) was designated as the self-regulating body for advertising content regulation in both broadcast and non-broadcast advertising.

OFCOM's current regulatory duties do not extend to the regulation of internet-based content. There's little international law to govern online use or abuse, however, the EU and US governments are working upon joint legislation to control the internet. Recognizing what is and isn't acceptable behaviour across international and cultural boundaries is extremely challenging.

The potential for handset theft means security is a key issue. Whether you're developing m-comms for others or your own company you have responsibilities regarding privacy and security. Hackers can transmit viruses via your mobile and sell on stolen data. The law has tended to lag behind developments in new technologies hence you need to diligently provide security measures to protect your brand and your users.

Environmental impact on m-comms

As we take a greater interest in our environment, driven by the media and better education, the need for you to consider the environment in a friendly and sustainable manner is important. We'll discuss this in detail in Chapter 9.

Ethical issues and m-comms activities

Privacy campaigners are concerned about the implications of the data and information available on mobile phones downloaded from SN sites, intranets, confidential meetings, etc. The potential for recording covertly in order to use the information in an unethical manner for commercial and profitable purposes poses problems. Many professional bodies provide Codes of Conduct, which we'll discuss later.

Facebook landed itself in hot water over plans to use information on their users for commercial purposes. The users weren't aware that their dialogues were being listened to and analysed. In response to the backlash, Facebook had to quickly review their plans. As a general rule you should always seek the permission of those you're observing. As mentioned earlier, the security and privacy of the data on sites is a 'hot' issue. You need to carefully consider what information you collect and how you collect and use it, otherwise you could potentially land yourself in ethical trouble.

Taking British Airways (BA) as an example organization, apply the PEST framework to the company. What are the current political and legal issues currently affecting BA? Are their any current or potentially new economic issues or changes they need to be aware of? What about any cultural or social issues? Are changes in technology going to affect this organization? How?

By doing this exercise it is easy to see just how complex the marketing environment can be and how numerous the issues are. Once you've had a practice, try to apply the PEST framework to your own organization.

Consider your situation (II) … Activity 17

How do you identify future threats and/or opportunities? Make a list of what sources/resources you can use to monitor all of the forces in the macro environment. Consider how frequently you monitor what is happening, say, in the economy. Encourage your staff to access quality sites via their mobiles, eg timesonline. Then introduce procedures to ensure it's done regularly, eg once you've identified an opportunity… what next? What happens to the information that's gathered? This information should drive changes.

The micro environment

The micro environment (Figure 5.1) involves those stake-holders in and around your company over whom you have some influence. As the world changes, so do the stakeholders with whom you interact. Every change can have a knock-on effect with what, and how, you communicate. The degree of influence you can exert varies from stakeholder to stakeholder. You have the most influence over your staff and (with social media sites) the least over the users.

Marketing is about not only satisfying the customer but also delighting them. It's about adding value, quality and innovation to their experiences but in an ethical and socially responsible manner. Just think about what happened to Woolworths in the early 2000s. This retail giant took their eye off their core customer, whose needs were changing. New online competition entered the market and Woolworths struggled to adapt. They suffered tremendous losses leading to over 800 store closures. This is sad enough, however, they were also the key supplier of CDs to retailers across the UK and the lack of stock in the crucial Christmas period brought a number of companies down. Woolworths has now risen from the ashes, initially online then in the high street. It's a new business model and I for one hope it succeeds.

FAQ: Why focus upon the customer and not concentrate on core organizational strengths (winner of the longest question award)?

The company's core strengths should indeed be identified and you need to know that:

- they add value for the customer;
- they are difficult to imitate;
- they provide potential access to a wide variety of markets;
- they link internal skills with resources such as technology.

That said, it's customers who purchase your products in exchange for money. This exchange brings you and the customer together. If the customer has a positive experience they will tell their family and friends. If it's a bad experience the chances are that they will tell even more people about it!! This applies now more than ever with the advent of new technologies. Web 2.0 has seen an explosion in the use of smartphones to access user websites (see www.imdb.com), blogs and social network sites.

Customers are also constantly changing and technology is enabling quicker, easier decision making. For example, consider the cost-comparison websites such as Kelkoo or Pricecompare.com. As customers change, their desires, needs and wants also change and if your company doesn't adapt with them, you'll start to dissatisfy the customer and lose them to the competition.

That said, you will have to assess your strengths and weaknesses before you implement any marketing-related changes. Some of the tools you can use are:

- Balanced Score Card;
- Boston Control Group (BCG) Matrix;
- Core Competences Model;
- Stakeholder Analysis (customers, competitors, suppliers, distributors, publics);
- Porter's Five Forces;

- 5Ms (Money, Men, Machines, Materials, Markets... some people include Minutes);
- Value Chain Analysis (VCA).

TOP TIPS

 These tools are well covered in other texts.

 Consultants are readily available to help you.

ACTIVITY

 Many to Many communications, such as social networking, are increasing in importance from a marcomms point of view. Whilst these sites provide additional opportunities, there are inevitable downfalls to consider. Start tracking some of the communication messages on social networking sites. It may give you an idea of how content and use of tools differ over time and circumstances.

CHAPTER 6
HARVEST KNOWLEDGE

How to use m-comms as a research tool

MOBILE COMMUNICATIONS AND RESEARCH

Real value can be added to your company's knowledge and decision making by using m-comms as a research tool. You can use it to:

- provide valuable information from colleagues;
- listen to your advocates, consumers, bloggers, etc to find out what they're saying about your company, brands, campaigns or competitors;
- test out new concepts/ideas;
- help shape your strategies.

CASE STUDY

Facebook and Nielsen tested an online research tool that measures the effectiveness of adverts. The tool, Nielsen BrandLift, placed opt-in polls on Facebook users' homepages that gauged their attitudes to adverts on the site and measured their purchasing intent. The frequency of polls was controlled to prevent users being asked to participate too often. Nielsen said that no personally identifiable information would be collected. The surveys were placed in positions where users saw sponsored messages.

Facebook's chief operating officer Sheryl Sandberg said 'The combination of our unique ability to quickly and effectively poll a sample of our more than 300 million users and Nielsen's expertise in data analysis will give marketers access to powerful data they can use to understand and improve current and future campaigns.' And that Facebook 'wants to be the first place marketers turn to when they want to engage consumers'.

Business history is littered with examples of ill-prepared communication campaigns for product launches or repositioning efforts failing due to a lack of research. Carrying out good quality research is undoubtedly the best way to prepare for any marcomms strategies that you intend to undertake as it provides the information you need to make the most appropriate decisions.

Harvest knowledge... Activity 18

Using well-sourced information reduces risks by creating more certainty when making decisions. List the business decisions you make on a daily basis. Some may be fairly minor, others with far-reaching consequences. How many of your decisions are made using intuition, based on past practice, imposed from above or use good data? Map these out in terms of high, medium and low importance.

As we are all well aware, there is often a variety of answers or solutions when making decisions.

MARKETING RESEARCH

One of the first factors to consider is that the term 'marketing research' is very broad and encompasses many different 'types' of research such as:

- Market research – can focus upon the key features of the actual market in which you operate: the market, market size, volume or value of the market. Particularly useful when considering brand new markets for entry.

- Product research – the product, product features or desirability of the product. Often used in NPD. Can also be used to counter any product-related problems, eg falling market share. Third parties such as business schools or consultants can minimize political fallout.

- Distribution research – where the products ought to be sold or where the customer wishes to purchase the goods.

Social network-driven m-marketing is the new search marketing as it allows marketers to connect with consumers on a large scale. Increasingly, marketers are looking at SN sites as places to advertise to targeted audiences, with hundreds of such sites and millions of users worldwide.

It's vital that you truly understand the focus of your research, what information you require and what problem you are trying to solve. Even if you have the resource and choose to employ a marketing research agency, you still need to understand the process that research goes through. Why? Because you'll need to respond to the data once it is presented to you.

Research by its very nature is systematic and often follows a logical approach (Figure 6.1).

FIGURE 6.1 The systematic marketing research process

Be as specific as you can about the problem you wish to address. This is key as it provides focus to the research project. If your research problem is too broad you'll struggle to gather useful data. Alternatively, if it's too narrow you could miss key information. It's important to understand at this early stage whether you require qualitative or quantitative data – or perhaps the use of both, which in reality is often the most suitable course of action. However, the choice is governed by your problem and chosen research objectives.

Quantitative research

This refers to collecting numerical data that generates statistics to analyse. It's usually gathered when you're seeking an answer that's representative of a larger population.

CASE STUDY

When psephologists Ipsos Mori carry out research to predict UK general elections, they often use quantitative data that seeks to represent the whole voting population. They typically poll a sample of 1,500–2,000 prospective voters and generate results that are accurate to $(+/-)$ 3 per cent. When it's a close run thing 3 per cent may not be accurate enough and they'd need a much larger sample or alternatively they can triangulate their findings with other surveys. Phone surveys are now the most common form of political poll and subsequently more research is being carried out via mobile phones.

Qualitative research

This refers to collecting 'soft' data based upon people's attitudes, opinions, feelings or perceptions. Often how we feel is a greater force than how we logically think. Qualitative research is often used to ascertain consumers' feelings regarding new products or services.

CASE STUDY

Research doesn't have to be big, however. Twitter allows real-time research, for example one wine merchant organized wine tasting at multiple locations and asked the 'tasters' to tweet their responses to each wine. The merchant then analysed the results, which were detailed and provided useful feedback.

Generally speaking, researchers tend to collect secondary data before primary data because it already exists. Sources can be internal, ie company reports, or external sources, eg government publications or directories. The internet enables secondary research to a greater extent than ever before although its scale is problematic with recent estimates of 65 billion pages in the web. Disadvantages of secondary data are that it is neither specific to your research question nor is it up-to-date nor particularly accurate. It can, however, give you a feel for the optimum direction.

Also, secondary data is cost-effective (as it already exists), relatively quick to collect and you don't need to be a skilled researcher to collect or use it. However, the use of secondary data will only get you so far and you may need data specifically focused upon solving your research problem and objectives, which you'd collect for the first time – aka 'primary data'. Primary data is specific, relevant, timely and if collected and analysed properly, accurate.

Data collection techniques or methods

There are different ways you can collect primary data using mobile technology. These involve varying degrees of skill due to the range of methods available. The most common methods in consumer research are quantitative questionnaires and qualitative focus groups and interviews.

Questionnaires are very useful if you need to collect data from a large number of people. You will need to question a representative sample of your target audience. Always remember the more people you question in your target audience, the greater degree of accuracy your results will have, however, resource limitation may hinder you. Questionnaires can be administered in a number of ways:

- face-to-face with either self or respondent completing;
- telephone (mobile or land-based);
- post;

- e-mail;
- online, eg pop-up.

In-depth interviews are a useful way to collect qualitative data of a sensitive nature. They involve only one respondent and the interviewer can probe for in-depth answers, feelings, opinions, etc. Traditionally, interviews have been regarded as costly, however, the results often justify the investment. That said, smartphones (with video and audio capture facilities) are increasingly used to interview people in remote locations. A future development will be the use of smartphone-enabled video-conferencing that will enable groups of people to be interviewed simultaneously.

Bias

Each technique has strengths and weaknesses. You need to acknowledge these to avoid bias, which is the bane of good research. You must consider the sensitivities of both the researcher *and* the respondent. Hence some questions would probably be better asked in a non-face-to-face way, eg via mobile phone.

CASE STUDY

The following comes from a Market Research Society (MRS) 'Research' bulletin: 'Today, a lesson in the importance of questionnaire wording. According to a CBS/*New York Times* poll, 70 per cent of Americans support "gay men and lesbians" serving in the military. But when it comes to "homosexuals", it's a different matter – only 59 per cent are in favour of them serving. The Obama team will no doubt be scratching their heads to see if they can get an 11-point poll lead on any other issues just by re-arranging the words.'

Remember, raw data is not the same as information. Once you have collected the data you then have to analyse it. Quantitative data is easier to analyse as it's well suited to statistical analysis, spreadsheets or simple graphs. Packages such as SPSS can help you to carry out complex analysis of large amounts of data. Qualitative data must also be analysed to identify themes and trends. Simply offering a few respondent quotes isn't usually enough.

Rest assured that good knowledge gained from well-designed research can only strengthen your company's position, so don't be surprised if others find the results interesting as well. Put effort into making the report stand out. A common mistake is that researchers and marketers make the report easy for themselves, not the reader. Provide your report in a mobile-friendly format such as PDF.

Ethical marketing – permission marketing and beyond

Marketing research is at the heart of most marketing decisions. To remain competitive, innovative and attractive to the customer, we must constantly evolve our products, services and organizations. Marketing Research is central to providing us with the data and information to help us to do this successfully.

Harvest knowledge... Activity 19

Download the MRS Code of Conduct (from http://www.mrs.org.uk). It gives invaluable insights into how to conduct research as well as providing guidance for conducting research in an ethical fashion.

I can't stress this enough – you *must* be able to identify your most important, valuable customers and e-loyalty research can help you to identify them. In B2B selling one of the great buzzes is finding a small account and then developing it into a key account. How do you categorize this nascent account? Also these days the marketing environment is moving at such a pace that many of the old labels are too static.

TOP TIP

Those of us who have spent many years selling to customers would add that your sales force is an invaluable resource.

ACTIVITY AND QUESTIONS

As a first step ask the following:

- Who are your most valuable customers now?
- Who will be your most valuable customers in 18 months time?
- Who will be your most valuable customers in 3 years time?

The results should tell you a lot about your strategic direction, not to mention your sales team. These simple questions should inform your e-strategy (as well as your offline strategy).

CHAPTER 7
NURTURE
GROWTH

Before Web 2.0 buyers had limited options for learning about your services and/or products. Largely, this made marketers' jobs easier as they built brands from the top down using mass communications, such as trade advertising, press releases and targeted tactics such as direct mail.

M-COMMS AND BUILDING BETTER RELATIONSHIPS

The advent of user-generated communications has shifted the emphasis (from simply closing the deal) to helping consumers to make decisions prior to the purchasing decision itself. Companies must adopt a more customer-centric approach if they wish to 'sell not tell'. It's the most exciting time there has ever been for starting and growing companies and you can tap into this as long as you recognize how customers' roles have changed and the need to add value for customers. Answer this... are you now engaged in trying to sell what you think they want? Or is it a case of finding out what information consumers need to make better decisions?

The Decision Making Process or DMP

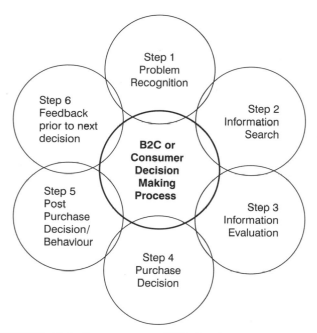

FIGURE 7.1 Consumer or B2C (business-to-consumer) decision making process

Historically, marcomms campaigns sought to encourage customers to buy products, ie close the deal. Marketers often simply listed the product's features without relating benefits, ie how they helped solve customers' problems. Pre Web 2.0 this may have been enough but these days online consumers expect much more than just the traditional transaction, they expect service, reliability, website personalization, easy use and fun… the thrill of the auction is a key element of eBay's business model.

Bear in mind that the time dedicated to the various stages differs due to whether the purchase is a routine purchase or something of higher risk where if it goes wrong the implications may be long term. Every stage of the DMP presents opportunities for prospects or customers to seek opinions or input from a blog, forum, social network and/or comparison sites.

Nurture Growth... Activity 20

Your company can use m-comms to shape the dialogue so that customers make the right decision... ie buy your goods and services! This means communicating with other stakeholders who influence the 'buyer'. Using Figure 7.1 identify where you can exert the most influence with your m-comms tools. Ask your sales people to use the model with your customers. You'll gain valuable insights and be able to better focus your marcomms.

The Decision Making Unit or DMU

The stakeholders within the DMU are:

- initiator;
- decider;
- buyer;
- user;
- influencer;
- gatekeeper.

The stakeholders interact and influence each other... sometimes energizing each other, at others restricting each other. In SMEs different stakeholders can have multiple scenarios, eg initiator and user. Post Web 2.0 the DMU still applies, however, different stakeholders not only fulfil differing roles, they often contribute to online debates via a forum (or indeed multiple fora), blogs, social network sites or comparison websites. A further complication is that these stakeholders may also use multiple media channels simultaneously – such people are known as media multi-taskers.

Nurture Growth... Activity 21
Following from Activity 20 identify the actors In the DMU and how you can exert influence with your m-comms tools. Ask your sales people to map out their key clients. Remember different stakeholders want different information, eg stakeholders often seek information of a technical nature.

Customer satisfaction

As exchanges bring suppliers and customers together, relationships are formed and you need to develop the initial relationship by finding out as much as you can about the client's needs. Put simply, if you give customers what they want, they'll return to buy your goods and/or services. Servicing existing customers is much cheaper than attracting new ones, therefore customer satisfaction enhances sales turnover and profitability as well as increasing your market share.

Satisfied customers not only tend to be repeat buyers but also tend to tell their friends, families and colleagues. Conversely, if they have a poor experience, they tend to tell even more people about it!! You probably now better understand the need to move away from single transactions and towards effective management of long-term customer relationships.

Word of Mouse (WoM)

As previously discussed Word of Mouth is the strongest form of promotion and has now morphed into Word of Mouse (WoM) on SN sites. If your brand garners negative publicity the WoM can pass around the world in seconds. You have to assume that your customers and prospects search online, particularly on SN sites where they can read 'unbiased' peer comments, prior to purchase, hence the top-down approach is increasingly inappropriate. Promoting your company via SN sites can contribute, with good WoM, to a personalized 'pull' method, where users are encouraged to take an active role.

CASE STUDY

In early 2009 Innocent Smoothies sold a 20 per cent shareholding to Coca-Cola and sparked an SN-inspired media storm. For 10 years Innocent received positive reviews due to practices such as using organic materials and donating profits to charity. This positive brand equity didn't prevent hundreds of negative comments being posted on Innocent's website. Although you can't keep all of the people happy all of the time, the power of blogs and SN sites when in tandem with other media such as newspapers created fallout that had to be managed. Innocent wrote to their customers stating 'we will be the same people making the same products in the same way. Everything that Innocent stands for remains in place.'

Using a mobile platform to acquire customers

You have to make it easy for the visitors as there's a high likelihood that non-converts may never be seen again.

Nurture Growth... Activity 22

Design your m-comms so they catch the Attention (of prospects) by creating a favourable impression. Find out what Interests them. Ensure that your products create some prospect Desire – make it fun or offer free content initially. Then provide the information needed for the prospect to make the right decision, ie take the Action of ordering from your company.

The next stage is to change first-time customers to repeat customers. Remember, it's considerably cheaper selling more to existing customers than it is acquiring new ones. You need to consider your approach for migrating existing customers to online customers (see Figure 7.2). This depends on your starting point, ie whether you offer traditional and/or online provision.

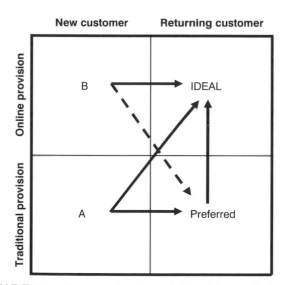

FIGURE 7.2 Approaches for relationship marketing

Assume your company has converted a prospect into a customer traditionally (A) or online (B). The first transaction (A or B) is fraught with risks and you must ensure everything is done to 'get it right first time'. Eventually, after they've ordered from you several times, they'll forgive the odd mistake, however, in the early days new customers are easy to drive off. Remember, responding to a mistake says more about your company than when things go smoothly.

Also, not all returning customer positions are equal as your overheads are likely to be considerably lower online. Being pragmatic means having repeat customers in any form is 'Preferred' to single transactions (hence the dashed migration from B to Preferred). Ultimately whether through single (A or B to Ideal) or multiple migrations (A or B to Preferred to Ideal) you have an opportunity to migrate them to the 'Ideal' position where they're happy to buy online and you enjoy the healthiest margins.

Some practical steps you can take are:

- Divide your contacts by heavy or light smartphone usage, time slots, information seekers, etc.

- Target your m-comms towards timing-driven users with messages such as 'sale ends at 9 pm'.

- If you've established permission use Bluetooth to highlight bargains when users are within proximity of the supplier.

- Send time-related messages when most likely to affect their behaviour, eg when people are leaving work to remind them to stop on the way home.

- Keep messages short so that they are easily read on mobiles.

- Provide notices, e-vouchers and regular, say, monthly newsletters – they need to be suitable for computers but still be readable on mobile devices.

- Link your m-comms to your other marcomms, eg establish whether they sometimes access emails on their mobile phone. Look to segment your mailings with increasing accuracy to target mobile e-mail readers as a distinct group.

e-CRM

Customer Relationship Management (CRM) is regarded by some as the solution to many marketing problems, whereas others regard it as the cause of many of the problems. Simply put, having an enormous database of contacts is not a guarantee of success. Rather, CRM can provide the platform so you can use m-comms to serve and nurture customers over their lifetime rather than in a single transaction. This makes good business sense as existing customers are, on average, five to ten times more profitable.

Nurture Growth... Activity 23

Good CRM can provide enormous benefits. For more information and access to useful white papers have a look at the CRM Today site (http://www.crm2day.com).

Chaffey (http://www.davechaffey.com) argues that e-CRM is packed with fundamental common-sense principles; surprisingly, many companies do not adhere to them. Those of us who constantly promote customer centricity aren't that surprised that many companies misuse their data. Users of sites such as Facebook generate enormous amounts of data and you'll need to manage the data to produce information effectively and efficiently in order to make knowledgeable decisions, hence CRM programmes undoubtedly have something to offer... but they're no substitute for genuine customer insight.

Customer Satisfaction Management (CSM) is a different approach that well lends itself to m-commerce. As customers change, their desires, needs, wants and information requirements also change. If your company doesn't change and adapt with them, it's likely that you'll start to dissatisfy customers and suffer attrition to the competition. Hence it's not enough to simply amass a huge database – you have to massage it to ensure the information you extract from the data is good enough to support your decision making and knowledge management.

Adding value – myth or reality?

More than ever before, m-comms provide the opportunity to find out what consumers think as well as the networks and communities of users, prospects, friends, colleagues and even families. Brands can no longer dictate to customers if they seek to promote community-orientated engagement marketing. In this scenario a fundamental question that you *must* ask is 'Where is your company adding value?'

Is it adding value internally or in the customer's perception (which ultimately is the only 'added value' that means anything). You may need to consider the key question: Who provides the insight – stakeholders in the micro environment or customers? If you get this wrong your company may be wasting substantial funds. With m-comms-driven real-time sites such as Twitter this information may evaporate before you've had the chance to act so you may need to change how you monitor the environment.

Life Time Value (LTV)

Since Web 2.0, users have been generating content much of which has related to goods and services. Unlike the old days of marketing when you simply built a brand and promoted your product (whether customers were listening or not!) you're now expected to build customer relationships by communicating with (rather than at) them. It's not enough to simply satisfy customers, now you have to communicate with their communities.

You won't be able to control all aspects of the communication process (think herding cats or juggling soot and you won't be far off), however, the benefits to all parties are there to be seen. They are happier as they want to be heard. You are happier as you can use their feedback to tailor your service provision. It's a win–win!

Increasingly, users access social network sites such as MySpace, Facebook and Twitter via the mobile platform. These sites provide perfect forums (or fora if you prefer!) for your dialogue. Many companies do this poorly so you have what Chaffey (http://www.davechaffey.com/) describes as a golden opportunity for integrated CRM to create competitive advantage. Hence everything you do should be geared-up to seeing the customer's LTV (ie the sum of their contributions to your company over a long timescale) rather than a single transaction.

> Say a client spends £100 every other month. Do you treat it as a £100 transaction or as potentially £12,000 over the next 20 years? Every time you interact with the client imagine a figure of £12,000 hangs on the service provision and your whole approach will move towards relationship marketing.

Taking an LTV approach will improve your chances of satisfying customers. That said, loyalty is not the same as satisfaction. Hence it makes sense to consider steps to improve e-loyalty.

e-loyalty

Ellen Reid-Smith (2009) suggested a Seven-Step e-Loyalty Consulting Process as follows:

1 clearly establish e-loyalty goals and objectives;
2 identify the Most Valuable Customers (MVCs) and their loyalty drivers;
3 develop a strategy to create an intelligent dialogue with customers;
4 design a web offering to fulfil on MVC's loyalty drivers;
5 formalize an e-loyalty programme for MVCs;
6 persuade customers to want a relationship;
7 develop feedback and measurement tools.

These steps are largely common sense, however, theory and practice are not the same thing. The tricky bit is persuading customers to want a relationship, which you can only do with continuous dialogue (see Figure 1.1). You must sell the benefits and not simply list the features – sadly this happens far too often. Customers want to know how you can help them to solve their problems. Your success will come down to implementing this customer-centric approach and this approach needs support from the top of your organization.

Advocates

We previously discussed how Opinion leaders and formers can play a key role in your marcomms. This is trivial compared to using m-comms to enable existing customers to become advocates for your company (see Figure 7.3). You know when you're really looking after and satisfying your customers when they start 'selling' the benefits of your company to their friends, family and colleagues.

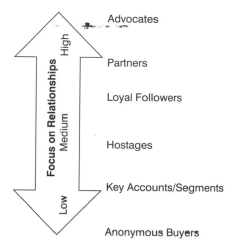

FIGURE 7.3 Relationship marketing continuum. Adapted from Piercy (2009)

Advocates promote your goods and services for no financial gain to themselves and when someone you respect and/or care for extols the virtues of a product you'll pay far more attention than if the manufacturer said exactly the same thing. This 'non-marketer dominated' communication is as good as it gets from a marketing perspective.

It's similar to opinion leaders, however, advocates carry even more weight as they've bought your goods with their own money – in other words they've taken the risk. Also, they have existing relationships with the people in their communities and advocates can boost your sales and profits while improving customer attraction and retention, not to mention staff morale.

Partners

If you use intermediaries in your channels you should view them as partners in your business. Time and resource needs spending on developing and strengthening your relationships. Trust and confidence should be central to long-term relationships however, if you choose to design and use a one- or two-level channel, conflict must be avoided at all costs.

m-comms, internal marketing and building relationships

We introduced the notion of internal marketing in Chapter 4. Internal marketing (see Figure 4.1) is a well-established concept that is often poorly practised. Effective internal marketing needs senior management commitment, which sadly isn't always provided. You may need to sell the benefits of change to your colleagues or get them to see the big picture if customer service expectations are to be exceeded and not just met. M-comms can help promote internal marketing as they can provide instant feedback on whether internal customers are 'buying' your communications and what influences these processes.

Every communication represents an opportunity to show your company in a positive (or negative) light. Understanding internal customers' needs and having their best interests at heart sends a powerful signal. That said, not all stakeholders are equal, hence you need to be aware of the impact your communications could have. Obviously, care is needed when communicating with internal stake-holders. Although not all stakeholders are equal, they all have the capacity to create issues that will need effective solutions.

TOP TIP

Having a better grasp of your own drivers, you'll be better placed to understand how stakeholders react to your communications, and be able to provide useful information and resources to facilitate their decision-making.

ACTIVITY AND QUESTIONS

Ask yourself the following questions: Why are you working in the manner that you are? Why are you attending particular meetings? What have you gained from the interactions you've had with colleagues? What have you learned that's new? How have the meetings moved things forward (if at all)? How do your internal relationships compare with those that are external? Do you communicate in a different way? Can m-comms be used to improve your internal communications?

CHAPTER 8
EMBRACE
CO-ORDINATION

Remember, your marcomms tools (Figure 3.2, page 45) don't stand in isolation. Rather they need to be blended to provide the best support for delivering your message to your customers. The choice of tools has a direct impact upon the effectiveness of other management tools.

IMPLICATIONS FOR MANAGEMENT

To illustrate this let's consider the use of m-comms with the PLC (refer to Figure 2.2 on page 22). Remember PLCs are getting shorter and, when launching new products, your company needs to penetrate the market as quickly as possible. There's little time to recoup your development costs, break even and start to make a profit! Also, every product is different as is every related PLC. Hence the opportunities for m-comms are almost limitless, but let's consider the three scenarios depicted in Figure 2.2.

Zone A Your company is spending money developing and testing the product prior to release. Here you'd carry out mobile research with prospects or users of existing models. Remember, a single text message, or tweet is meaningless; but a collection of them can be analysed and produce valuable information.

If it's a high-value product you'd target opinion formers with a view to inform the early adopters. You could marry the research with a mobile teaser campaign to raise awareness while the research is ongoing.

Zone B Your product has launched successfully and you want to extend the rapid growth so as to recoup more of your R&D costs. You may use Twitter or generate a mobile e-mail campaign to liaise users' clubs. In either case, you'd seek testimonials explaining the benefits they've had from the products.

You'd aim to feed positive feedback via the mass media as well as informing your customer base, ie those clients who've so far held onto their old models. You could simply advertise, however, that's expensive and the impact is diminished as people expect you to say good things about your own products. That said, they'll gladly accept the word of real customers or other opinion formers.

Zone C It makes sense to keep sales in the maturity section at as high a level as possible for as long as possible. This is known as extending the maturity section and there are varying m-comms techniques that will help you to do this. You'd use PR to explain the reliability of your products. You'd recycle good feedback from organizations such as Which?, social network sites, user fora, comparison websites and so on. If at all possible you'd want this to get into the mass media so you may seek a new angle.

Embrace Coordination... Activity 24

Draw the PLC for one of your products then apply the lessons from above. Where can you use m-comms and other tools from your extended marcomms mix to communicate with key stakeholders? Which tools can generate feedback? Which ones are for raising awareness, etc?

SYSTEMS

Professor Malcolm McDonald argues – in his excellent book *Malcolm McDonald on Marketing Planning* (2008) – that marketing in the UK has gone backwards in the last 10 years. I think this may be due to companies being too inward focused as well as having 'systems' that don't add value for the customer. Let's consider systems in more detail.

Your company is made up of different systems that interact with each other and their respective environments, for example CRM systems. Your success depends on how well these communicate and interact with the internal and external environments (see Chapter 5). You won't be shocked by the notion that many managers protect their systems jealously and lack a vision of the bigger picture. Certainly too many managers are process or systems driven when they should be customer driven. This may be due to the nature of modern managers who work at a hectic pace and too much of what they do is unstructured, unplanned and unco-ordinated. You need to ensure that your managers can cope with the fragmented, hectic nature of the modern business environment. A way to support your managers is to improve your marketing planning.

MARKETING PLANNING

McDonald argues that 'the purpose of marketing planning and its principal focus are the identification and creation of competitive advantage'. If the lack of marketing planning is a serious concern in your company you're strongly advised to read McDonald. In the meantime this chapter will consider how the mobile platform can support your marketing planning (Figure 8.1).

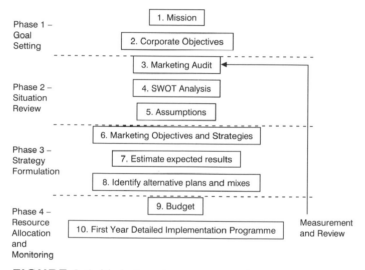

FIGURE 8.1 Marketing plan.
Adapted from McDonald (2008)

The key thing is to look as far forward as is sensible. As discussed earlier, PLCs are crashing and you may need to plan for 18 months rather than the 3 to 5 years that people usually associate with 'strategic' decisions.

Gap analysis

The hardest part can be knowing where to start! A common way to address this is to carry out a gap analysis. A gap analysis illustrates where your company is now and forecasts where your company will be after a period of time. If the forecast is simplistic and the resulting target unachievable this will cause problems. Too often the sales target is a wish list – 'it's where we need to be'. Larger companies often measure success in terms of turnover but care is needed. If your sales are up 50 per cent in three years you may well be delighted, however, if the market has grown 100 per cent in the same timescale you've got a problem. You've lost market share to your competitors and this could have dramatic effects. Growth in profit is often safer but market share is better.

You may elect to measure your success against some other criteria such as brand awareness or customer satisfaction. These can be measured, but some skill is needed and you may want to use the mobile research platform as discussed in Chapter 6. Gaps have to be closed if you want to hit your targets. This can be achieved by reviewing the opportunities available to your company. Operational gaps can be filled by improving productivity, reducing costs or increasing prices. This links to earlier discussions on extending the maturity stage of the PLC where you would seek to stimulate sales or find alternative uses of existing products.

Scenario planning

A successful marketing plan will also consider the problems that might occur and make appropriate preparations to deal with them should the need arise. This is a central factor in an organization's ability to respond to change through the planning for assumptions that do not come to pass, and identification of strategies to mitigate the impact of these unfulfilled assumptions in order to still achieve financial goals. Assuming you now know where you want to be the next key decision is how to get there. The stages in Figure 8.1 can be condensed into the following:

1 Goal Setting – Mission Statement and Corporate Objectives;

2 Situation Review;

3 Strategy Formulation;

4 Resource Allocation and Monitoring.

Let's briefly consider each of these key stages.

1 Using Mission Statements and Objectives to set achievable goals

A mission statement should reflect your company's purpose, why the company exists, how it operates, what sort of company it hopes to be. The better ones define the benefits offered to customers. It should fit with the values and expectations of your key stakeholders. Companies that have unclear mission statements often have employees who lack direction. Employees need to engage with a progressive, aspirational, grounded vision of the company if they're to be fully motivated to drive through any changes.

Embrace Coordination... Activity 25

Mission statements can be inherently political with stakeholders seeking to 'empire build'. To reduce the risk of this use m-comms to ask your staff 'What should your mission statement be?' Light blue touch paper and retire!

The core elements of a mission statement are as follows:

- purpose;
- long-term view – strategy;
- area of company involvement – products or services;
- key strengths;
- benefits to customers;
- policies – standards – attitudes, eg Corporate Social Responsibility (CSR);
- value systems, eg fair trade.

Embrace Co-ordination... Activity 26

Use your m-comms to inform customers that your purpose is to solve their problems and add value for them. Inform them of your mission statement – incorporating all or some of the above.

Larger organizations' corporate objectives are often set in terms of profit, since this will satisfy (usually remote) shareholders. With SMEs it's usually the owner/manager who needs to be satisfied and this is often shaped by their personality or attitudes. Objectives can only be chosen after an honest assessment of your (company's) attitude to risk. Do you speculate to accumulate or would you rather go for organic incremental growth? If you're risk averse you don't want to plan for huge growth as high risk, aggressive approaches can take you furthest away from your existing strengths and capabilities.

Identifying key objectives provides a platform and achievable goals for your marcomms activities; they are most effective if few in number, concise and SMART (Table 8.1).

TABLE 8.1 SMART objectives

Objective	Comments
Specific	avoid being either too vague or too tightly focused
Measurable	always ensure you can measure the success of the objective
Accurate (some say aspirational or achievable)	don't set a wish-list as nothing demotivates staff more quickly than imposed targets that can't be met
Realistic	how probable is it that the objective will affect changes?
Timely (some say targeted)	depending on resources; identify the time your objectives need – may mean modifying, simplifying or being more specific with your objectives

Examples of objectives might include:

- raising your profile;
- altering the attitudes and opinions of key stakeholders;
- increasing your market share.

You'll probably need to use a variety of tools from your comms mix (Figure 3.2) to achieve your objectives. If your attitude to staff using mobiles to tweet is 'you're supposed to be working' you may want to think again. Use m-comms such as tweets to overcome corporate resistance by encouraging regular contributions. Tweets are quick, informative and may help deliver the message that it's customers that count.

Your communications will need to be co-ordinated throughout your business. This is known as co-ordinated marketing communications or CMC. You'll seek the ideal blend of comms tools to create effective campaigns. In doing so, wider audiences may be reached, more consistent messages can be delivered and there is a greater chance of penetrating the *noise* and being remembered!

2 I am reviewing the situation

Ok, so it's a quote from *Oliver*! But it still applies. You can't move forward until you know where you stand. This applies to companies of all shapes, sizes and age. A common mistake among SMEs is that they take an ad-hoc approach to planning. This is a schoolboy error!!

So you've produced a forecast and you've a good idea where you want to be. Before you can start you need to identify what you do well, as well as areas for improvement. This can be done with a marketing audit, which helps you to monitor internal and external factors that affect your company. Effective marketing audits should be:

- detailed;
- structured;
- independent; and
- regular.

Once you've audited your micro and macro environments (see Chapter 5) you can then enter your findings into a SWOT analysis (Figure 8.2).

S(trengths) and W(eaknesses) are snapshots of your organization over recent years and up to the current time. They're inward focused, historical and seek to identify information that will help you to be more effective and efficient. O(pportunities) and T(threats) are external and

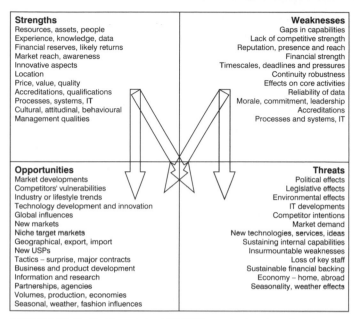

FIGURE 8.2 Populated SWOT analysis showing how elements interact

future-based. Having scanned the macro environment they are how you see the issues that will affect your company in the near future. SWOTS can be:

- used for strategic planning (eg entering new markets, investment opportunities, etc);

- marketing planning (eg product development and launches, research, etc);

- from departmental or individual perspectives;

- looking at what you deliver to whom and how you do it.

If done regularly SWOTS can help you to spot trends before others, thus giving you an edge. Also, you'll be in a better position to make improvements, eg you may need to make better use of resources. Alternatively, the skills-base of your company could need improving. SWOTs can identify patterns and trends that will influence your marcomms.

Embrace Co-ordination... Activity 27

Using Figure 8.2 as a template and any information gleaned from the activities in Chapter 5, populate a SWOT for one of your target segments or, if a larger company, a strategic business unit (SBU). It should be detailed and include trends rather than snapshots.

At this point you're now ready to consider your strategic choices.

3 Strategy

Since we're talking planning (potentially) years ahead the thorny issue of strategy arises. The word strategy is often abused. In *The Apprentice* you'll often hear the candidates saying 'our strategy is to...'. At this point I'm usually screaming at the TV that it's tactics not strategy... unless I'm wrong and the tactic of selling bunches of roses the following day really is strategic... I suspect not.

Key strategic areas that m-comms can affect include:

- supporting major change;
- communicating management messages;
- communicating the business mission/vision/values;
- raising awareness of business issues and priorities;
- raising and maintaining the credibility of the management;
- employee motivation;
- allowing for staff to feedback;
- improving the communications skills of management.

Tesco recognizes the value of its employees, stating that they are as important as customers with regard to the success of the business. They regularly ask staff what is important to them, and respond accordingly; treating them with respect, providing managers who help them, creating interesting jobs, and an opportunity for progression. In return Tesco's staff are fully aware of the company's objectives through its 'Every Little Helps' strategy. Tesco understands that if its staff have rewarding jobs, they're more likely to go that extra mile to help customers.

Strategies are the broad methods chosen to achieve your objectives. They don't include details of courses of action that will be followed on a daily basis – these are tactics. It's important to understand how strategies differ from tactics.

Typical strategies could be:

1 SO1 – raising your profile in the media by engaging more with journalists as part of a media campaign;

2 SO2 – boosting product sales or service take up, eg increase podcast downloads;

3 ST1– engaging more mobile users with your online newsletter;

4 ST2 – creating a mobile platform to educate your staff on new products;

5 WT1 – to develop a social media campaign to target so far unreachable youth segments.

You could easily identify a wide range of strategic options, hence you'll need to prioritize which ones best suit your company. This is done with a TOWS analysis (Table 8.2).

TABLE 8.2 TOWS analysis

Strategies	Urgency	Probability	Impact	Total
SO1	3	3	3	9
SO2	3	3	2	8
SO3	3	2	3	8
WO1	2	2	2	6
WO2	2	2	1	5
WO3	2	2	1	5
ST1	3	2	3	8
ST2	2	2	2	6
ST3	2	1	1	4
WT1	2	2	1	5
WT2	2	1	1	4
WT3	1	1	1	3

When teaching CIM students the TOWS step is often the game-changer, ie the step where everything falls into place. As discussed previously, CIM students come from all walks of professional life. If they find it useful I've no doubt you will too!

Embrace Co-ordination… Activity 28
Using your SWOT from Activity 30 carry out a TOWS analysis and identify three key strategies that can utilize m-comms.

4 Put your money where your mouth is!

Controls must be established to assess how well your marketing plan is being put into practice and, again, m-comms can make this easier and more accurate. Three key factors are:

- There should be scheduled opportunities to reflect on the plan's effectiveness.

- All stakeholders should be aware of the timescales and encouraged to 'feed back' via the mobile platform either in the form of messages, a social network site or a blog.

- You will need to be seen to act on these reflections.

Embrace Co-ordination... Activity 29

If you're worried that employee's tweets may take up too much valuable staff time you can measure twitter behaviour using resources such as www.tweetstats.com and www.twitterholic. com. These allow managers to see the volume of tweets by week, day or even hour. They also allow you to monitor retweets and replies. In doing so you'll be able to follow key trends, identify new issues... as well as who are the biggest twitterers.

You can also invite consumers or users to voice their concerns regarding how your company performs. They'll provide a key insight into areas such as a lack of staff knowledge, training, vision, skill, security, noise, etc. Hence tweets and m-comms can be tools to promote learning within your company.

One of the key benefits of m-marketing is the ability to review your marcomms quickly. Hence the effectiveness of a campaign can be viewed immediately and if necessary amended. Reports can be produced in a simple spreadsheet and can cover key metrics (Table 8.3).

TABLE 8.3 Key mobile metrics

	SMS	MMS	WAP
number of messages sent	☺	☺	☺
number delivered	☺	☺	☺
number bounced	☺	☺	☺
number of stop messages	☺	☺	☺
number of replies	☺	☺	☺
number of downloads and value		☺	☺
number of opens and click throughs		☺	☺

SMS (Short messaging service)
MMS (Multimedia messaging service)
WAP (Wireless application protocol)

Budget

In a strategic marketing plan there should be a detailed budget for the early part of the plan. The budget needs to be related to what the whole company wants to achieve. The results can be broken down into the different market segments, therefore allowing analysis of how well the marketing mix has worked on specific target sectors. Ideally your company should use the budget to contribute to knowing the Return on Marketing Investment (a variant of ROI). It makes sense to know the marketing costs associated with differing strategies.

SMEs AND PLANNING

Marketing planning is an essential activity, however, many SME owners deem it unnecessary. They regard marketing as something more relevant to large organizations. If in doubt SMEs should seek external advice – their local business school will often be able to provide cost-effective assistance.

It's impossible to apply a single rule to all SMEs – they're simply too diverse. Many exhibit entrepreneurial behavioural patterns while having little structure, whereas others are long-standing and well-established, with structures comparable to larger companies. Whatever the scenario, it will impact on their approach to marketing.

USING SUPPORT MECHANISMS

A wealth of good advice is freely available simply by tapping into the Codes of Conduct of various bodies. If you're adopting a code of practice to improve ethical behaviour (see Chapter 10) you'll find they:

- focus on regulating individual behaviour rather than the company en masse;
- require formal documentation;
- tend to target specific areas, eg gifts, anti-competitive practices, etc;
- expect employees to sign up to the code thus shifting responsibility from the management;
- tend to be developed from third party codes;
- tend to mix moral and technical imperatives;
- often simply describe existing practices and may not offer solutions to problems.

Third party codes naturally focus on differing aspects, eg the Market Research Society provides a comprehensive code available from their website (www.mrs.org.uk). This covers any ethical research-based issues you may have.

The Direct Marketing Association (DMA) provides an excellent guide entitled *Mobile Marketing Best Practice Guidelines*, which covers collecting and managing data, mobile campaigns, measurement and reporting. Have no doubt that at times dealing with consumers can be difficult and the guide refers to tricky areas such as adult content, complaints and dispute resolution. It describes how the UK-based mobile network operators have created a joint code of practice for the self-regulation of new forms of mobile content, addressing parental concerns about inappropriate or adult content being sent to children's handsets. A copy of the code of practice can be obtained from the Independent Mobile Classification Body (IMCB) website (http://www.imcb.org.uk/classificationframe/). The DMA suggests that when setting up a mobile campaign you need to ensure that:

1   the customers have given permission to communicate with them specifically via this medium;

2   you're clear about the data being used (preferably make sure that it has been collected in-house or that the exact collection methods are known);

3   the medium is appropriate to that specific offer/target group (what is trying to be achieved – how will mobile support it?);

4   the message is appropriate for the medium (can it be communicated by text or via images);

5 any cost to the consumer can be justified and is clear in the communication (remember that they pay to send messages and can be charged to receive any acknowledgement – or 'bounce back' – message, so make clear that they understand the full cost to them);

6 the consumers understand that any downloadable content within your campaigns (eg ringtones or wallpapers) is reliant on the compatibility of their handset and also how it will be charged;

7 you are clearly identified to the mobile user;

8 your message includes the ability for the user to opt out from further messages.

And finally

Many managers have struggled to adapt to the relentless changes in technology. Naturally, operations have to keep pace with changes and the move to m-marketing could be one such change. What is needed is not change for its own sake but the right change.

TOP TIPS

You'll need to reflect on …

 The balance between efficiency and effectiveness

 Attitudes to/and relationships with mobile customers

 The balance between our needs and wants

Redefining customer satisfaction

 Refocusing onto the long term objective, rather than shorter or medium term

 Rethinking the value chain

 New corporate culture

ACTIVITY

 In order to embrace coordination you need to find the right balance for your company, target segments, marketplace etc. Too little detail will lead to a lack of action whereas too much could lead to 'analysis paralysis.' A lack of skills and resources are key factors that lead not only to poor marketing planning but also to ineffective implementation. It's not enough to carry out a marketing audit and then simply sit on the results saying 'that's that done for another year.'

QUESTION

 Has it become a ritual, an onerous task? If so it's unlikely to have the required impact. Remember being efficient means doing tasks right whereas being effective means doing the right tasks.

CHAPTER 9
WHERE DO YOU STAND?

SUSTAINABILITY AND MOBILE MARKETING

Let's be clear, you must not only match your products/services with the needs of customers but you also need to ensure that you provide customer value. Increasingly companies are expected to be profitable while also looking after the environment and their people – this is known as being sustainable.

FAQ: Is sustainability a real concern for businesses?

This is a key question. Events like the Y2K bug (where the world didn't come to an end and yet companies spent billions) can create a degree of cynicism and/or scepticism. This is often referred to as green-washing and companies who have lied about their environmental credentials have often incurred the wrath of the online community.

Starbucks has done much good work with charities and yet it was lambasted for having running taps. When they subsequently moved to exclusively using Fairtrade coffee some cynics suggested it was mere green-washing. Those of a pragmatic disposition recognized that Starbuck's adoption of Fairtrade products would indeed make a great contribution to the coffee producers. Starbucks could not be accused of resistance to change, which is often the case. It's possible that they suffered from poor consumer education. Consumers are often imperfectly educated and companies need to embrace m-comms as a means of redressing the imbalance. Starbucks should use texts, pictures, videos and mobi websites to provide a continuous supply of stories that clarify how they're improving the lives of the coffee producers.

So, you need to run your business profitably and you recognize the need to be more sustainable... how do you start?

Well first you need to adopt a sustainable marketing stance (see Glossary for definition) and then use m-comms to ensure that all stakeholders are aware of your position. Clear communications are essential as sustainability 'ownership' can be fuzzy in some companies and hotly contested in others. Corporate Social Responsibility (CSR) is often controlled by Human Resource departments. Some organizations recognize the importance of CSR with elements in their mission statements (a strategic management decision) that may include 'green' issues (possibly a quality control issue), ethical supply policies (the purchasing department) and charitable links (all of the above!!).

This corporate 'bun-fight' is reflected on the political stage where pro-sustainable development bodies differ widely in terms of what to sustain or to develop and when. In B2C sectors you could argue that responsibility lies with the service provider, the consumer, the community, the regulator or even the government. An example of governmental influence is the Companies Act (2006), which heavily impacts CSR. Increasingly, the environment will be used as a launch pad for governmental initiatives and legislation. Having an m-comms platform could be invaluable in terms of informing the different parties, responding to feedback and managing expectations.

Previously (in Chapter 8) we discussed how useful third party codes of conduct can be in helping you to act ethically.

Where do you stand?... Activity 30

If you're still faced with resistance from internal stakeholders, use your mobile platform to draw their attention to some of the indices and initiatives that are widely used to help companies measure their sustainability. You can use m-comms to provide the links or alternatively disseminate information to your stakeholders. Three such sources are:

- The Dow Jones Sustainability Index (http://www.sustainability-index.com/);

- The FTSE4Good index (http://www.ftse.com/Indices/ FTSE4Good_Index_Series/index.jsp);

- The Global Reporting Initiative (http://www.globalreporting.org/Home).

These provide credibility to the argument for being more sustainable while acting as valuable sources of information in their own right. The FTSE4Good index, for example, includes human rights criteria. You could sell the concept of sustainability to cynics by highlighting how the public's mounting concerns are partly driven by:

- growth in prosperity;
- expansion of media coverage;
- notable disasters;
- greater scientific knowledge;
- longer term cultural shifts;
- PR and celebrity endorsement.

Most of these have increased as a direct result of increasing mobile communications. With four billion users worldwide it's difficult to keep bad news under wrap. Celebrities are now as famous for their tweets as much as their prime activity (Stephen Fry is an honourable exception). You may argue that this is all well and good but does it really affect your business. Well, let's look at some of the implications. The following are increasing on a daily basis:

- levels of environmental awareness/concern leading to demand for eco-friendly products, adoption of green product substitutes, reuse/redesign/recycling of products;
- consumer values are shifting from consumption to conservation;
- demand for less pollution from industry with more conservation of resources and energy saving;
- greater regulation by government with businesses charged for environmental impact of their activities;
- demand for, and availability of, information on environmental issues with companies

expected to conduct and publish ecological audits;

- opportunities to develop protection of the natural environment, animal rights and endangered species.

As you can see, pressure is increasing on companies to act sustainability.

Where do you stand?... Activity 31

There are an estimated 1,400 environmental pressure groups in Britain alone. Any one of these groups could go to the press and create a serious situation where your brand could be damaged. The 13 largest green groups in the UK have over five million members who may exert pressure through lobbying, PR campaigns, direct action, partnership and consultancy involvement. As discussed in Chapter 5 you need to map these groups in terms of their interest in your company against their ability to cause problems. Once mapped use your m-comms to engage them in dialogue and try to reduce their impact in the mass media.

Many of these people believe that modern business practices advocate 'selling more' whereas 'sustainability' is about consuming less. You may need to adapt your m-comms to address these concerns. Meet them head on by inviting them to contribute questions for you to answer – mobile technology is ideal for this. Make sure you inform the local media of any good news stories that result from these dialogues. Sustainability is not simply about damage limitation; rather it's an opportunity for you to promote your good practices.

WHERE DO YOU STAND... WHERE DO YOUR CUSTOMERS THINK YOU STAND?

The 'Triple-Bottom-Line' (TBL) is increasingly replacing the traditional bottom-line by including social and environmental responsibility. Your company must be able to position itself effectively if you seek to make good strategic, tactical and operational decisions. Hence you need to reflect on where you're perceived to stand in terms of sustainability (Figure 9.1).

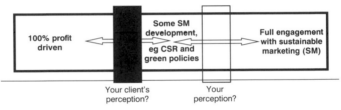

FIGURE 9.1 The sustainability continuum

Obviously such tools are limited in that companies are complex and dynamic hence it can only be a snapshot. That said, it's the vital first step.

Where do you stand?... Activity 32

Carry out a poll of your staff and customers asking two simple questions:

1   How do you rate your company in terms of sustainability?

2   How do your customers rate your company in terms of sustainability?

If your perception is 8/10 and your customers rate you as 5/10 then you have a problem! You may be at a disadvantage – your competitors could exploit this!

You need to know where you stand. If you have a poor rating you need to consider what's stopping your company from adopting sustainable SN marketing practices.

Using m-comms to overcome barriers to adopting sustainability

In future you'll need to operate in an increasingly sustainable fashion and you'll need to identify and remove barriers to adopting sustainability such as:

1 multiple stakeholder interests with hidden agenda and interests;

2 shareholder dominance;

3 definitional problems leading to lack of clarity regarding responsibility for sustainability;

4 overly sales-oriented;

5 short-termism, eg excessive focus on dividends over longer term investment.

Although it's unlikely that all of these apply to your company, you need to consider some of the factors. First we need to be honest. Your organization will face challenges in moving to a more sustainable position. The CIM recognize key issues as being:

- costs;
- technical and organizational;
- conflicts between objectives;
- international implications;
- lack of visibility;
- timescale;
- lack of certainty about the nature of the problem;
- concerns regarding proposed remedies;

- tokenism;
- moral fatigue.

These can all cause problems, particularly when you consider that some issues, say costs, can combine with others (say timescales) to create barriers. What's needed is a mobile campaign that regularly updates your stakeholders with measurable evidence of improvements. Don't expect them to make huge leaps in the dark. Instead gently nudge them over a period of time and you'll be amazed at the progress you make.

FAQ: How will I know if I'm making good progress?

This is a good question as changing your marketing isn't as easy as many people think (see Chapter 2). The CIM argue that all businesses, no matter how big or small, new or old, should measure themselves against their competitors. A well-established way of measuring yourself, and therefore seeing how you've improved, is through benchmarking (see Glossary for definition).

Benchmarking

It's a practical and proven method to help you measure your sustainability performance against your competitors. Remember, positioning is simply about how your customers (and prospects) perceive your company in relation to the competition. Benchmarking can be used to instil best practice into your company across a range of issues, however, in this case we're concentrating on addressing your positioning (Figure 9.1).

You'll be able to improve your understanding of the key sustainability issues by comparing and contrasting data across your business activities, functions and sectors. Benchmarking will provide the springboard for your strategic planning (as discussed in Chapter 8) as you'll need to address the issues highlighted within the benchmark report. It's highly effective in identifying and disseminating best practice in sectors and networks. As always, you'll have choices in how you approach this; namely, with or without external help.

Doing your own sustainability benchmarking costs you nothing but your time, although you'd be wise to read widely around the topic before you start, speak to your local business school, study a relevant course or even pay for a few hours of coaching from a professional.

Where do you stand?... Activity 33

If you want to develop your benchmarking skills the CIM suggest the following resources:

- The Benchmark Index – formed by the Department of Trade and Industry in 1996 and run through Business Link. Compare your businesses with others (http://www.benchmarkindex.com/).

- Best Practice Club – an organization to facilitate co-operation and information dissemination on benchmarking and best practice (http://www.bpclub.com/).

- Director's Briefing on benchmarking – quick guide to what it is, what it can mean for your organization and how to plan/implement benchmarking (http://www.bizhot.co.uk/files/St4bench.pdf).

- BuyIT – best-practice network for the information, communications, telecoms and e-business industries. Has links to actual best-practice guidelines and case studies (http://www.buyitnet.org/).

So what should you benchmark?

You'll need to consider where you want your company to be on the 'Sustainability Continuum'. You may choose to commit to a greater or lesser extent. Figure 9.2 suggests a framework that will help you to benchmark your company in terms of Sustainable Marketing.

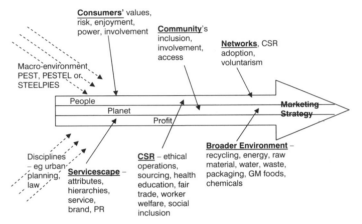

FIGURE 9.2 A framework for sustainable marketing

The factors portrayed can impact on multiple TBL elements, for example adopting a CSR policy as part of SM could impact on people and profit. As can be seen, benchmarking sustainability is hampered by the multidisciplinary influences. Research has shown distinct differences, for example, between how urban planners (who have shaped much of the sustainable development debate) and marketers define sustainability. We live in fast-changing times and it's not surprising that a variety of terms are used to represent new, emerging theories. Critics of marketing suggest it's only interested in the (short-term) selling of products to the target group. Ironically, this outdated notion (aka sales orientation) is now considered a contributory factor in consumers' awareness of green-washing and is largely decried by sustainable marketers.

If you want to use outside support your choices are to employ an environmental or sustainability consultant or agency. You can employ them on a one-off or ongoing basis. It should be a continuous process but you may want to test the water initially (no pun intended). Don't expect instant results as it can be a slow process. Greenscope is an environmental benchmarking tool offered by Brunel University in conjunction with retail developers. Ultimately it aims to help retailers to change consumer behaviour. They anticipate a retailer's move to a green marketing strategy is likely to take up to five years to complete and their approach is based on detailed consultations. So be patient.

Once you've carried out your sustainability audit you can publish the results in a mobile format that's easy for people to assess (Figure 9.3).

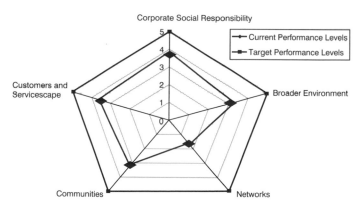

FIGURE 9.3 A polar diagram showing results of sustainability benchmarking

Some of the measures you introduce will satisfy one of the TBL foci but many will cross over.

Where do you stand?... Activity 34

You could reduce your carbon footprint by reducing attendance at meetings and/or conferences by asking those involved to follow mobile debates using 'hash tags' (see Glossary) to make it easy to follow the thread. Hence these meetings could be a considerable environmental improvement undertaken at virtually no cost.

Figure 9.2 shows some of the areas where you can improve your environmental impact. Smart companies are linking, say, recycling into rewarding customers. Let's consider some examples of how the TBL bottom lines, namely People, Planet and Profit can energize each other. The following examples illustrate how Airmiles and Arcadia linked mobile phone recycling schemes with improving repeat business.

CASE STUDY

Planet Example 1

In 2009 Airmiles launched a mobile phone recycling programme where members collect 'miles' by recycling mobiles. Their website has an interactive element in the form of a calculator informing members of how many miles they'll collect up to a total of 750 airmiles. The scheme is being managed by ShP Limited, an e-waste recycling company. The phones are reconditioned with all profits being reinvested into environmental projects.

CASE STUDY

Planet Example 2

Highstreet group Arcadia, which includes Topshop, Dorothy Perkins and Wallis, has teamed up with Mopay.co.uk to turn old mobile phones into gift cards. Mopay is an online mobile phone recycling service that offers consumers cash in return for unused handsets, which are refurbished and sold on in developing countries at lower costs. Users receive vouchers that can then be redeemed at any Arcadia store. By 2010 the service has paid out £2.6 million to consumers and over £1 million to charities since launching in 2006. The scheme helps improve communications and infrastructure in developing nations.

It's incidental that both companies recycle phones, what matters is that with both examples there are clear gains for acting more sustainably. Both organizations:

- receive a tangible benefit, ie consumers are encouraged to repeat purchase with vouchers;
- use the expertise of a specialist recycling partner;
- gain positive PR from the by-products, ie improved environmental projects and helping developing nations respectively.

Fundamentally there's nothing wrong with this. You have to take a pragmatic approach and although some of the more 'principled' dark greens will object the recipients in the developing nations will be delighted with the support. You may need to use the mobile platform to improve your internal marketing in order to overcome such resistance. Remember, sustainable marketing needs to be 'sold' on the basis of future gains. You can use m-comms to:

- build bases for understanding by disseminating information;
- co-create plans for the implementation of sustainable marketing;
- make sure people are aware of your financial commitment;
- demonstrate managerial commitment;
- encourage participation and contributions throughout the company;
- sustain internal PR programmes creating healthy responses to sustainability ideas.

What about the message?

It's worth revisiting the notion of the 'message'. All digital channels are subject to the same noise problems as traditional media so how you develop your message is no less important. You still need to start with the story. There is no point getting carried away with the variety of new and exciting mobile channels if the message doesn't deliver. You need to consider whether consumers will be prepared to spend time on the content and assess its 'stickiness' factor. Remember you are no longer in control! The higher the 'talkability' factor, the more likely people will be to engage and pass on to others. So creativity will remain at the heart of a good mobile campaign. Agencies will continue to play a pivotal role in m-comms development as they adapt and adjust to the challenges and opportunities of social media.

Charities

Today, businesses are more like charities with published ethical and sustainability platforms, whereas charities are more like businesses with professionally run marketing campaigns.

However, marketing generally, and particularly research, are weaknesses for charities and many acknowledge the need for change. They need to market themselves in a co-ordinated way rather than rely on their usual ad-hoc approach.

That said, charities have always been willing to adopt a flexible approach to marketing and income generation, with staff often having the freedom to develop activities in effective and efficient ways. Today, charity managers are under increasing pressure to meet stakeholder expectations, hence it is appropriate to consider them in more detail.

Most people use charities in some way and the sector makes a substantial contribution to the UK economy, with over 200,000 registered charities generating a turnover of over £32 billion while employing almost 600,000 paid staff. Many charities became over-dependent upon external funding, which often diminished their long-term marketing planning. In these days of changing funding, financial security is often no longer guaranteed. Vital services have been under threat because of changes in European Objective grants and the Single Regeneration Budget. The EU expanded to 27 member states and new members are attracting more funding. This confirms the need for charities to monitor the micro and macro environments (as discussed in Chapter 5).

Corporate citizenship

You can create a mobile-comms campaign highlighting positives from your audits as well as how you're going to implement changes where needed. Remember corporate citizenship refers to the relationship between companies and society – not just the local community, but all of the stakeholders in your micro environment. Whether you call it 'corporate citizenship' or 'social responsibility', the act of becoming progressively more sustainable will help you in the long run. Mae Lee Sun (see Activity 35) offers eight tips to get you started on an environmentally sustainable marketing plan:

- Become fluent in sustainability; understand how it relates specifically to your product or service – if you aren't aware, your customers won't be either.

- Educate your customers; show the practical value and benefits of what is being offered and why it's worth a higher price.

- Use clear language that conveys a positive image of your product or service.

- Be wary of sending contradictory messages and 'green-washing.' Are you advertising your company as 'green' with little to back it up? Are you endorsing environmental causes merely to boost your company image? If so, you're likely to be found out.

- Highlight environmental progress and programmes your company has in the works. Companies of all sizes have become popular models of corporate excellence for the environmental/sustainability initiatives they have in place.

- Invite consumers into the dialogue – ask for their feedback and not just on the product but on how you serve them. Consumers want to know whether you're socially responsible too.

- Network with other green-based businesses. Green business alliances are being established and are becoming certified as green by entities such as the American Consumer Council.

- Green it if you mean it. Offer the best product available because it makes sense and if you want everyone to benefit in the long term.

Where do you stand?... Activity 35
Have a look at Mae Lee Sun's site (http://maeleesun.
com/2008/08/22/green-marketing-8-tips-to-get-you-started-on-
an-environmentally-sustainable-marketing-plan/). It has useful tips
and guidance.

It could be argued that 'business' is part of the problem not
the solution. On the contrary, business needs to be at the
forefront of the 'sustainability' debate as trade takes place
between and within business organizations and not governments. Sustainable marketing is an evolution of being marketing orientated and largely uses the same frameworks and
tools as conventional marketing.

TOP TIP

You will have to adapt...

The information you use to make your decisions

The criteria you use to measure performance...
sustainability audits may be required

The company values, mission and/or vision statements
with which marketing objectives must fit

The extent to which marketing is the responsibility of the
whole organization

FIGURE 9.4 The four Ss of sustainable marketing

ACTIVITY

In Chapter 8 we discussed how your mobile strategies must be enshrined in your company mission and/or vision statement. Figure 9.4 could act as a template where you can insert the appropriate information in order to represent your new sustainable positioning. Remember a picture tells a thousand words – apply the diagram to your company and use your mobile platform to send it to all involved.

CHAPTER 10
WHERE DO YOU STAND (II)?

Nowadays, accelerated technological change is the norm. Also, many of the newer technologies of the 'noughties' will converge.

WHAT DOES THE FUTURE HOLD?

Increasingly, mobile technology will provide the platform for new business models and Web 2.0-driven m-commerce will be one of the largest business opportunities of the next decade. The opportunities are there for companies of all shapes, sizes and age. You'll have to be ready to react and may have to take risks by launching new products (Figure 10.1).

You need to assess the degree of risk and how you wish to be perceived by the customers. Hence we'll discuss some of the new mobile developments and you'll be able to consider how the future could look for your company. Remember things tend to come and go quicker in the digital world.

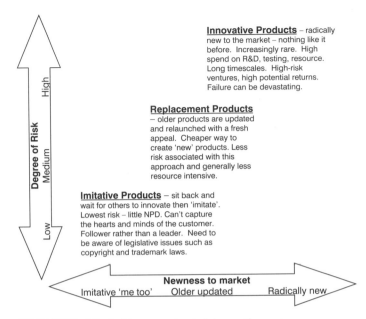

FIGURE 10.1 New product risk continuum

In 2009 Facebook had over 120 million active users, however, fewer users were logging on and once logged on were spending less time on the site. So if you are considering investing in advertising, PR, etc on an SN site, what you deem to be a medium to channel your goods and services to millions of intended receivers, may not be as effective in the mid to long term. You need to monitor the volatile technological environment and move swiftly to take advantage of opportunities and also minimize any potential threats to your business and brand.

CASE STUDY

Apple's iPhone advertising campaigns increasingly pushed the convergent nature of their product, ie it's a multi-use tool rather than simply a phone. This shift in consumers' perceptions of smartphone usage has serious considerations for other industries and some companies saw opportunities to enter new markets. In December 2009, online estate agents Rightmove's shares dropped more than 10 per cent in one day when Google announced a potential website for 2010 where estate agents could list properties free of charge. Even the suggestion of such a site was enough to drive the incumbent's shares down. When Google (the new entrant) announced their iPhone sat nav app in 2009, shares in existing providers fell sharply.

Where do you stand? (II) ... Activity 36

As discussed in Chapter 5, you must monitor your environments. In this case are there apps in circulation or being developed that could affect your company? How would you find out?

THE CYNIC KNOWS THE PRICE OF EVERYTHING AND THE VALUE OF NOTHING

Oscar Wilde couldn't have imagined that his observation was going to be highly relevant over a hundred years after his death. In this case the cynicism applies to the young generation of consumers who don't understand why they should pay for online services such as films, music, books, apps, etc. When asked how artists should make a living the young consumers usually suggest that they tour or sell more books (assuming they're hard copies or one assumes the students would pirate them as well!).

Some artists have anticipated these developments. Robbie Williams's deal with EMI is based on a share of all of his revenues, including touring and merchandise. Well that's OK for Robbie but what about young and upcoming bands? Also, what about songwriters? This is not just a UK phenomenon. In fact, in parts of the world copyright laws will continue to be flouted with tacit support from the respective governments.

CASE STUDY

Chris Anderson discusses how piracy accounts for an estimated 95 per cent of music consumption in China, which has forced record companies to rethink completely what business they're in. There is a large, lucrative Chinese music market... for ringtones less than 20 seconds long! China Mobile, the largest carrier, reported more than a billion dollars in music revenues in 2007. As goes China, so may go the rest of the world. Record sales in the USA fell by nearly another 10 per cent in 2008, and the bottom is nowhere near in sight. The day may come when many labels simply capitulate and follow the Chinese model, letting music go free to become marketing for the artists, whom they monetize in non-traditional ways, such as endorsements and sponsorships.

It's not only young consumers who won't pay. The economic hardships of 2009/10 saw a reported rise in thrift. Some consumers have always found free material to be attractive and now a whole industry provides this – the open source software sector. Inspired by the great Sir Tim

Berners-Lee (who invented the internet as we know it and then gave away his intellectual copyright) and with a whiff of Californian anti-establishment thinking you can now run your PC without paying for a thing. Open source software will eventually combine with 'cloud' computing where you simply draw on software when you need it… completely legally! You'll recognize many of the names, eg Mozilla, AVG, Zone Alarm, Spybot, Java, Flash, Adobe, etc, etc.

Google's open source operating system will follow on from Linux to fill one of the gaps in the free economy. Expect the shift toward web-based productivity tools such as Google Docs (also free) to accelerate. Consumers increasingly will use mobiles to:

- play free online games;
- listen to free music on Spotify;
- watch free video on YouTube or Hulu; and
- use Skype to ring friends around the world from smartphones.

Anderson (2009) argues that 'it's a consumer's paradise: the web has become the biggest store in history and every-thing is 100 per cent off'.

The danger is that really good sites won't be able to 'monetize', ie generate enough income and bottom-line. Three popular examples of mobile service providers that illustrate this dilemma are:

- Twitter needs income to cover bandwidth bills;
- YouTube struggles to match its huge popularity with revenues;
- Spotify is hugely popular and it's mobile provision may ultimately challenge the hugely profitable iTunes… assuming it can get its business model right.

THE NEWS MEDIA BATTLEGROUND

The times are indeed a-changing. Former fee-paying newspapers are now being given away free. Free papers such as the *Metro* are increasingly popular with young consumers despite largely recycling news stories and being heavily reliant on agencies such as Reuters and the Press Agency. Recent hard times saw long-established, esteemed companies such as Johnson Press pushing pay freezes with the resulting human resource management issues.

At the same time, new technologies such as smart-phones lend themselves to online material with increasing streaming to hand-held devices, eg BlackBerrys, iPhones, Kindles, iPads, even the Nintendo DS is now online. Research at Leeds Business School found 18- to 21-year-olds spend more time online than they do watching TV. So it's not a great leap to recognize that in future they'll get their news increasingly via their mobiles. That said, it's not all plain sailing. Chris Anderson describes how 'the news-sharing site Digg, for all of its millions of users, still doesn't make a dime'. Advertising is going to become a major battleground where content suppliers will become increasingly protective. There'll be no safe havens.

The battle for advertising revenue

In 20 to 30 years' time it's unlikely that the BBC will still be funded by licence payers. They have one of the world's most visited websites, however, their current funding means they'll be less able to compete with new technologies. Incoming new technologies, eg 4G phones, will increasingly lend themselves to online material with evermore streaming to hand-held devices, eg BlackBerry, PDA, Nintendo DS, Apple iPad, etc. The battle over whose site should be the gateway (and hence the major beneficiary of advertising and click-through revenues) will intensify.

NewsNow (aka NewsNow.co.uk) is the UK's largest RSS site and has been aggregating links to internet news since 1997. By 2010 NewsNow had links to over 31,000 news sources, including top news publications. Like many online organizations NewsNow relies on a combination of advertising, sponsorship and subscription revenues to fund its services. Its site generates over two million users monthly and receives more than 100 million page views per month. However, it has been caught up in a battle over revenues that will continue to rage as companies adjust to life after Web 2.0. It accused News International (NI) of undermining freedom of access to public information having been informed by NI that it may no longer link to any NI sites.

This meant NewsNow visitors were no longer able to view content on the Times Online site, which is undoubtedly one of the best sites available today. The blocking was implemented using the robots.txt protocol, a convention for requesting search engines, web spiders and other web robots to refrain from asking for pages from all or part of a website. In December 2009, NewsNow pulled many of its links to national newspaper websites following attempts by The Newspaper Licensing Agency Limited (the NLA) to impose a scheme that introduced the requirement to obtain permission and pay fees to circulate links to freely available web pages. The scheme has subsequently been referred to the Copyright Tribunal. NewsNow.co.uk is the founding sponsor of the Right2Link Campaign (http://www.right2link.org/).

Regulation

We will see more regulatory activity in social media. If it's like previous occasions it will feature disclosure of interest, codes of practice, protection of minors and offensive material. However, we are unlikely to see the restrictions on amount of exposure to commercial messages that we see in commercial TV. Just how easy it will be to police channels is debatable so self-regulation is likely to be a key dimension.

Sport

There is a naivety among some of those who are promoting the new technologies. The changes hoving into view will radically alter the way we consume services. It's not fanciful to foresee direct streaming of, say, football matches to smartphones in the ground and for those at home. They'll be able to:

- see replays and review contentious decisions;
- place online bets while the match is ongoing on an increasing number of items, eg the number of throw-ins or who is substituted;
- place orders for their food and drinks at half-time;
- tweet their views of the game 'real time' so a picture can be built up;
- liaise with resting players and back-room staff during the game, etc, etc.

This way the clubs will increase their advertising revenue. The trend of clubs going into administration will continue and will only heighten their need to improve their bottom line. Extrapolate this for all sports throughout the year across the globe and you'll see there's an enormous opportunity for companies to develop their m-commerce platform.

EDUCATION, EDUCATION, EDUCATION

As discussed in Chapter 1, in a world that's constantly changing many things are the same as they've always been. Take university teaching for example. There are over 120 universities in the UK alone, producing something like 300,000 graduates annually. If each undergraduate studies, say, 10 modules you can see where the attraction lies for developers. When you factor in the international market the figures are mind-boggling. India and China produce four million gradates per annum… each!

Future partners looking for opportunities to develop mobile compatible materials with universities can be assured that:

- mobile technology is going to be used increasingly;

- fees are going to continue to rise and students will seek value-for-money propositions;

- international students will have more choice regarding where they study;

- most UK students have smartphones, are becoming more discerning and increasingly see themselves as consumers.

The Open University operates mainly online and has had over 10 million downloads of its content via iTunes. This tells us that students are receptive to the idea and an industry designing e-learning tools will no doubt spring up to satisfy this demand. A substantial market will evolve for companies that can work with universities to develop compelling materials. Leeds Business School is a centre of excellence for Public Relations and is heavily involved with the Chartered Institute of Public Relations (CIPR). All students who enrol on the Masters in Public Relations are given an iPod and are provided with a constant stream of podcasts.

FUTURE 'TECH' TRENDS

We have to consider what will come next. Well, certainly users will have more choice as the mobile replaces the desk-bound PC as the main platform for e-commerce. Mobile phones will have more processing power than current PCs and will be able to communicate wirelessly with many devices. These devices will range from medical devices where your doctor will be able to monitor your heart using pads designed for smartphones; your house will have smart technology that will adjust to circumstances, ie switch the heating off if it's a warmer day than expected or switch the oven on prior to coming home.

Personalization and customization

Suppliers will increasingly seek to personalize their full and mobi websites in order to improve the user experience. iGoogle lets you create a personalized homepage that contains a Google search box at the top, and your choice of gadgets. You'll access it from your smartphone and have access to:

- your Gmail messages;
- headlines from Google News and other news sources;
- weather forecasts, stock quotes, movie showtimes, etc.

On top of this you'll be able to store bookmarks while 'mobile' giving you quick access to the sites when you're next plugged in.

The trend for customization will continue on a number of fronts. Mobile phones embedded in watches are already available. Increasing miniaturization means this trend (of embedding the phone) will be extended to clothing and possibly even jewellery. Bluetooth motorcycle helmets are old hat (sorry!) so don't be surprised if more clothing becomes integrated with technology.

Widgets, widgets, everywhere...

Widgets have established themselves as key tools online where universal standards for page construction exist. They're well established, with some commentators suggesting Trivia Blitz was the first widget launched in 1997 and went on to feature on 35,000 websites.

What is a widget?

Chaffey (http://www.davechaffey.com) defines a widget as 'a badge or button incorporated into a site or social network space by its owner, with content or services typically served from another site making widgets effectively a mini-software application or web service. Content can be updated in real time since the widget interacts with the server each time it loads.' There is some debate regarding how effective they are, however, if you're interested have a look at Snipperoo's site. It has a lot of useful information and practical tips.

Why are we discussing widgets here rather than, say, the Process or Presence sections in Chapter 2?

There's no doubt that widgets will play an increasingly important role as the penetration of smartphones increases. Widgets will make m-comms easier as the users won't have to plough through large amounts of data. Instead they'll simply click a button that will take them to their preferred destination or programme. That said, their use has been patchy largely due to the lack of standards and the need for widgets to be compatible across differing operating systems and mobile types. There is some agreement that companies new to the use of mobile widgets should consider:

- their aims and objectives;
- the means of distribution;
- the server-side support infrastructure; and
- the run-time environment.

The good news is that there are initiatives investigating overcoming the issues of multiple platforms. Using the tagline 'Write Once, Deploy Everywhere!' BONDI is looking to create mobile applications, eg widgets that are universal and future proofed... the sooner the better.

Where do you stand? (II) ... Activity 37

If you're interested, have a look at the following websites

- http://bondi.omtp.org/default.aspx
- http://www.omtp.org/

4G

The next generation of phones will have substantially more functionality than the current 3G versions. The bandwidths will be substantially better, the processing power and storage will continue to double every 18 months and downloads will take place at up to 100 MB per second. New ranges of applications will make the most of these developments particularly based on video, which at times still struggles under 3G. V-logging will increasingly replace traditional blogging where the users use their mobile sets in situ rather than sat at a desk. Mobile-enabled video conferencing will become commonplace as the camera and microphone technologies improve. Hence you'll be able to have more, better-quality interactions with remote colleagues while reducing your carbon footprint.

Video-sharing sites will increase dramatically similar to the picture-sharing sites such as Flickr that are still popular. The reduced time to download video will see a corresponding increase in piracy. South Korea has led the way in broadband speeds with 100 Mbits being common when most of the UK was at 4 Mbits. You'll not be surprised to note that when it only takes a couple of minutes to download a film the tendency for illegal copying and sharing increases hugely. This was the case with South Korea.

User-generated content

As the quality of recording increases we'll see more video-based mobile journalism via sites such as OhmyNews. YoSpace is similar to YouTube but contributors are paid each time their clip is downloaded. Their SeeMeTV has generated 12 million downloads since its launch and handed over £250,000 to contributors.

Tocmag is a free user-generated mobile content service. The BBC reported how it allows users to create their own 'Tocmags'; up to six pages of video, audio, text and images, which can be shared with the public through its website. Since the company's launch in November 2006 over a million 'Tocmags' have been downloaded. This service could be an ideal way for SMEs to 'dip their toes' into adopting more m-commerce practices. Also, it could easily be used to promote internal marketing by getting multifunctional teams to generate material for their colleagues to peruse.

Security issues

Mobile prices will stagnate or even come down. Hence the future of m-marketing will increasingly be tied in with the apps that are available for smartphones. Since mobile phones interact with other platforms, communicating seamlessly with many devices, they'll increasingly be used to protect users' interests at work, home and play.

Smartphones will be capable of storing biometric data such as fingerprints and retinal scans. These will be complemented by voice recognition. These features enable secure transaction billing and increasingly enable using mobile phones to replace cash.

The major mobile phone companies, eg Ericsson, launched a payment system called Payforit. The Payforit scheme provides a safe, trustworthy environment for mobile content purchases. The 'Trusted Mobile Payment Framework' rules define how merchants, accredited payment intermediaries and operators co-operate to make mobile payments a secure and seamless process. Further to developing trust in mobile payment, Payforit aims at creating transparency and ease of use for consumers. A set of 'screen style' rules govern how payment pages look and function, simplifying and securing how users purchase content via a standardized interface presented on their mobile phones. Similar schemes already exist, for example in Alaska consumers can pay for household goods by mobile. This trend could ultimately challenge the need for carrying credit cards as it would provide considerably more security and ultimately reduce fraud.

Ultimately it's hard to see how the credit card industry can survive (in its current form) as users will increasingly use their mobiles as their preferred choice of payment device. The banking industry will come round to this system as mobiles will provide greater security. The Chip 'n' Pin development dramatically reduced credit card fraud. Mobiles will take this further. It's a moot point but eBay's purchase of Paypal may prove to be the buy of recent decades. Their auction business may have approached its ceiling, however, online and mobile payment is going to grow and grow. You must ensure that your goods and services can be paid for (easily) using a mobile platform.

Mobile gaming

Gaming is a major driver for hard and soft technology platforms. Global income from mobile phone games passed $7 billion in 2008 and is expected to continue to rise long into the future. A substantial gaming sector is mobile gambling, which is also rising. With substantial sums of money being exchanged, security features will be enhanced in future smartphones.

Virtual worlds

Virtual worlds are interactive, simulated online environments, often in 3D, that provide alternative realities where users participate in fantasy worlds. In most worlds users create 'avatars' to interact with others within the world. Avatars, unlike those in James Cameron's superb film, are simulated versions of the users, who can adopt details, eg gender, name, physique, appearance, clothing, etc. Modern smartphones are increasingly using avatars; eg the LG GDS510 (aka the LG Pop) gives the user the option to view inbound and outbound m-comms by avatar rather than a traditional listing.

By 2011 it's predicted that 80 per cent of people online will have one or more avatar (van Nes and Wolting, 2009). As the fastest grossing film ever, one thing for certain is that nearly everyone knows the word avatar now and it'll lose it's geek image sooner rather than later. Virtual worlds allow members to alter, develop, build or customize their environment, so in addition to your avatar you can decorate and furnish a virtual apartment. Worlds also allow and encourage SN activity such as forming relationships, social groups, communities, etc. Virtual worlds exist for children (*Club Penguin*, *Roblox*), teenagers (*Dubit*, *Sims*), young adults (*Second Life*) and 'grown ups'.

Where do you stand? (II) ... Activity 38
It's worth having a look at www.virtualworldsreview.com if you're interested in targeting your marcomms and/or m-comms at any of these segments via the virtual world medium.

Some ways to integrate your marcomms are:

- buy space (land) and establish an interactive presence;

- pay to feature your brand or organization;

- run a competition or other sales promotion activity;

- create a branded world, eg with sponsored communities;

- sell products or services to complement avatar creation, eg Reebok trainers for avatars in *Second Life*.

3D and Augmented Reality (AR)

3D is happening with mobiles and its acceptance will be eased as TV manufacturers, satellite providers and movies increasingly use the technology. You may think that it's limited on mobiles but the quality and size of screen has increased year on year. There are apps designers already looking to exploit this stage. You need to consider if any aspects of your m-comms would lend itself to 3D.

So far, AR has had little penetration on mobile handsets, however, it's likely to benefit from the growing online virtual world. AR allows online data to be overlaid on views of the physical world. Juniper Research predicts AR will generate $732 million by 2014. Compared to the whole social media market this is small, however, it's sure to grow as more applications come online.

Where do you stand? (II) … Activity 39

An open source AR product that has caught on quickly is Layar. With it, mobile users can superimpose a layer of virtual reality over the real world as recorded on their handset. This could, for example, be a map of the local pubs or dentists or banks, etc, etc. Have a look at their site (http://layar.com/) and then think of how your company could benefit from such a layer. If it has potential contact a developer and you're off and running.

Mobile phones may be increasingly equipped with mini-projectors as has already happened with some video cameras. This facility will facilitate both the 3D and AR applications. Although it may seem like sci-fi today you can't help but notice how the iPad looks like it would fit easily on the *USS Enterprise*!! Certainly it's worth keeping an eye on these developments, particularly if you want your company to be perceived as at the forefront on m-commerce.

What about the familiar names?

Google will continue to challenge the market leaders, eg their Android operating system will become increasingly important. Twitter is the current 'big thing' but not that long ago so was Friends Reunited. Will Google's Buzz challenge Facebook? What will Apple come up with next?

If Google's proposed voice translation software comes to fruition you'll be able to ring anyone around the world and speak without an interpreter. For example, you speak English and your colleague (in Japan) hears Japanese. They respond in Japanese and you hear English. If this works it will revolutionize how businesses communicate.

Convergence

Here's the tricky bit. All of the above are going to be increasingly available on all platforms. TV will be available direct (and via on-demand) on more mobiles. The BBC is already one of the world's largest providers of catch-up services… which is a major headache for the advertising industry as the BBC will be ad-free for the foreseeable future. Users will increasingly surf via their TVs (with manufacturers already developing widgets for TV sets). Users will increasingly multi-task, ie use online, mobile, telephony, cable, etc… at the same time!! You'll need to be able to react to the challenges this will bring.

REFERENCES

CHAPTER 2: ENABLE CHANGE

Armstrong, M (2009) *Handbook of Human Resource Management Practice*, Kogan Page: London

Armstrong, M, Gosnay, R and Richardson, N (2008) *Develop Your Marketing Skills*, Kogan Page, London

CHAPTER 3: ACTIVELY COMMUNICATE

Fill, C (2009) *Marketing Communications: Interactivity, communities and content*, 5th edn, Financial Times: London

CHAPTER 4: CONSIDER YOUR SITUATION

Kotler, P, Wong, V, Armstrong, G and Saunders, J (2005) *Marketing Principles*, 4th European edn, FT Prentice Hall: London

CHAPTER 5: CONSIDER YOUR SITUATION (II)

Porritt, J (2005) *Capitalism as if the World Matters*, Earthscan: London

CHAPTER 7: NURTURE GROWTH

Piercy, NF (2009) *Market-Led Strategic Change: Transforming the Process of Going to Market*, 4th edition, Butterworth Heinemann, Oxford

Reid-Smith, E (2009) Seven-step e-Loyalty Consulting Process, online at http://www.e-loyalty.com

CHAPTER 8: EMBRACE CO-ORDINATION

McDonald, M (2008) *Malcolm McDonald on Marketing Planning – Understanding marketing plans and strategy*, Kogan Page: London

CHAPTER 10: WHERE DO YOU STAND (II)?

Anderson, C (2009) FREE: The Future of a Radical Price, Random House

DMA (2009) *Mobile Marketing Best Practice Guidelines*, Direct Marketing Association (UK) Ltd. Available from http://www.dma.org.uk/information/inf-practice.asp [accessed 31 January 2010]
http://www.payforituk.com/pages/news/news1.html [accessed 31 January 2010]

Tocmag online article http://news.bbc.co.uk/1/hi/technology/6340103.stm#4 [accessed 31 January 2010]

van Nes, J and Wolting, F (2009) *Another Perfect World*, C4 programme, broadcast 23 June, online at http://www.channel4.com/programmes/another-perfect-world

GLOSSARY

advergame A video game that is designed primarily to advertise a product, organization or viewpoint.

advertising A non-personal form of communicating a message that uses paid-for media to reach the intended target receivers.

AIDA model of communication A communication model that aims to obtain Attention, Interest, Desire and Action.

ASA Advertising Standards Authority is the independent body set up to regulate advertising and other forms of marketing communication.

avatar A computer user's representation of himself/herself. An avatar can be three-dimensional as in games and virtual worlds, two-dimensional as in pictures on SN sites or text-based as in chat rooms.

banner ad An image on a website used to advertise a product or service.

benchmarking The CIM defines benchmarking as a 'process of measuring producers, services, and practices against strong competitors or recognized industry leaders. It is an ongoing activity that is intended to improve performance and can be applied to all facets of operation. Benchmarking requires a measurement mechanism so that the performance gap can be identified. It focuses on comparing best practices among dissimilar enterprises.'

benefit The gain obtained from the use of a particular product or service. Consumers purchase products/services because of their desire to gain these built-in benefits.

blog A frequently updated diary/journal for public consumption.

blogosphere Sum total of all blogs and their inter-connections. The term implies that blogs exist together as a connected community via which everyday authors can publish their opinion.

BOGOF Buy one get one free.

BOGOL Buy one get one later – a more sustainably acceptable version of BOGOF where the user can return later to purchase the goods. This reduces waste while promoting repeat visits.

brand equity The value of a brand.

brand extension strategy The process of using an existing brand name to extend on to a new product/service, eg the application of the brand name Virgin on a number of business activities.

brand name Used for the identification of goods or services. Can be a name, term, sign or symbol. A well-managed brand should uphold certain values and beliefs.

brand repositioning An attempt to change consumer perceptions of a particular brand; for example, VW has successfully repositioned the Skoda brand.

break-even A point for a business where turnover is equivalent to all costs.

buzz marketing Word of mouth communications between consumers that can be delivered or enhanced by the network effects of the internet.

CIPR Chartered Institute of Public Relations – the largest professional body of PR in Europe.

citizen journalism   Where members of the public play an active role in the collection, reporting, analysis and dissemination of news and information. Also known as public or street journalism.

competitive advantage   Offering a different benefit from that of your competitors.

consumer-generated media   General activity on the web where consumers contribute their own content. Also known as user-generated content.

data mining   Application of artificial intelligence to solve marketing problems and aid forecasting and prediction of marketing data.

decoding   The interpretation of an encoded message by the target receivers.

direct marketing   The process of sending promotion material to a named person within an organization.

diversification   A growth strategy that involves an organization to provide new products or services. The new products on offer could be related or unrelated to the organizations core activities.

e-marketing   The marketing side of e-commerce. Features efforts to market and sell products and services over the internet.

encoding   The dressing of a message with signs, symbols and language that the target receiver can interpret and understand.

EPOS   Electronic Point of Sales – electronic devices (eg registers, scales, scanners, displays, etc) that can be linked to internal systems, eg stocks, and also customer databases, eg Tesco Clubcard.

extended marketing mix   Takes the traditional mix and extends it to include People, Process and Physical

Evidence. Used extensively in service organizations (also known as the 7Ps).

flaming   A popular pastime online. A flame is a hostile and insulting message posted online or e-mailed.

flash mobbing   The sudden gathering of a large group of people in a predetermined location to perform some brief action then disperse quickly. The term is generally only applied to gatherings organized via viral e-mails, SN sites or telecommunications. It is not applied to publicity stunts organized by PR agencies.

focus group   A simultaneous interview conducted among 6 to 12 respondents. The aim is to obtain qualitative information on the given topic.

hash tags   These are short messages used on social media sites such as Facebook that can be tagged with '#'. For example, '#realale is my favourite kind of #beer' would allow you to follow the thread for real ale and beer.

lean back channels   Term used to describe communication channels where the consumer plays a passive role. Television has traditionally been a lean back channel.

lean forward channels   Term used to describe communication channels where the consumer plays an active role. The internet is a classic lean forward channel.

long media tail   Represents the shape of the media curve that begins with traditional mass media channels with high reach such as television and flattens out with expanding channels such as SN sites and blogs, which have low reach.

macro environment The uncontrollable forces external to an organization. The acronym STEEL PIES can be used to highlight the external forces at play.

market position The perception of a product or an organization from the view of the consumer.

market research Analysing and collecting data on the environment, customers and competitors for purposes of business decision making.

marketing mix The tools used to implement strategic choices traditionally consisting of products, price, place and promotion (also known as the 4Ps).

marketing plan A written document that illustrates the marketing activities of an organization for a given period. The document should include an environmental analysis, marketing mix strategies and any contingency plans should an organization not reach their given objectives.

mash up Original material such as a video or an advert that is edited from more than one source to appear as one.

media The vehicle through which a message is transported to the target receiver.

micro environment A uniquely configured environment of stakeholders where the organization has a degree of influence. The micro environmental stakeholders include customers, suppliers, distributors, competitors, publics, facilitators, agents, wholesalers and other intermediaries. Not all stakeholders have equal power and/or interest hence they need to be mapped.

niche marketing The process of focusing resources and efforts on a particular segment.

noise Any distraction to the communication process, eg daily distractions, moods.

OFCOM   Office of Communication – the communications regulator.

opinion former   A person who through their professional expertise has influence upon others.

opinion leader   A person who through their social standing has the ability to influence others.

PDA   Personal Digital Assistant – digital devices that replaced hard copy diaries and Filofaxes. Products such as Psions and HP iPaqs were popular, however, the advent of smartphones has seen a rapid decline as most of the services are common in mobiles.

personal selling   Selling a product or services one-to-one.

pop up   An ad that appears in a window on top of the browser window in a website.

primary data   The process of organizing and collecting data for an organization.

product cannibalization   Losing sales of a product to another similar product within the same product line.

product life cycle   The life stage of a product; includes introduction, growth, maturity and decline.

public relations   The process of building good relations with the organization's various stakeholders.

pull marketing   Where high demand leads to customers seeking information on supply from the company/brand rather than the marketer seeking the customer. Some refer to this as 'reverse marketing'.

push marketing   The reality for most marketers where the communications are sent to the consumer via intermediaries and channels.

receiver   The consumer or user within the intended target market.

relationship marketing   Creating a long-term relationship with existing customers. The aim is to build loyalty by satisfying customers.

RFID   Radio Frequency Identification Tags. Originally used as stock protection and for pricing but increasingly used to monitor buyer behaviour, eg RFID fitted to trolleys can plot the precise movements of trolleys in-store hence identifying areas that suffer poor footfall.

sales promotion   An incentive to encourage the sale of a product/service, eg money off coupons, buy one, get one free.

search engines   A database of many web pages which then 'ranks' the results of a search term.

secondary data   Researching information that has already been published.

segmentation   The process of dividing a market into groups that display similar behaviour and characteristics.

sender   The person or body that sends a message to an intended target receiver.

stickiness   Using content on the internet to encourage users to spend longer on a site, visit the site more often or give more attention to the site.

sustainability continuum   A snapshot of a company's overall position in terms of sustainability based on the triple bottom line. Needs to be contrasted with consumers' perceptions of the company.

sustainable marketing   R Gosnay and N Richardson (2008, *Develop Your Marketing Skills*, Kogan Page) offer the following definition 'Sustainable Marketing (SM) is predicated on the tenets of the Triple Bottom Line. Hence SM decisions should be ethical and guided by sustainable business practices which ultimately are the only way to resolve the tensions between consumers' wants and long term interests, companies' requirements, society's long run interests and the need for environmental balance.'

SWOT analysis A model used to conduct a self-appraisal of an organization. The model looks at internal strengths and weaknesses and external environmental opportunities and threats.

test marketing Testing a new product or service within a specific region before national launch.

TOWS analysis The step that must follow a SWOT analysis. The key marketing objectives (SO, ST, WO, WT) are ranked in terms of Urgency, Probability and Impact. It enables better focus and prioritization on the key objectives.

triple bottom line Elkington's notion that the traditional economic corporate focus on Profit can be complemented with the new social and environmental foci of People and Planet.

viral marketing The use of pre-existing social network sites by marketers to spread brand messages and other related marketing content. It is derived from the self-replicating nature of computer viruses.

viral video seeding Strategic and targeted plan of activity that results in a video or series of videos going viral. This usually involves identifying communities that fit the brand then uploading the video across multiple platforms with the aim that it will be spread to like-minded people.

virtual world A computer-based, simulated environment that users can inhabit and interact with via avatars.

widgets Applications or 'gizmos' that help display and present information.

wiki   Software that allows the co-creation and contribution of knowledge on a particular topic by groups of people. Allows contribution and collaboration from a number of users.

word of mouth   Consumers pass on information, opinions and feedback about brands and companies. Typically, a consumer tells five or ten friends then the communication fades. This is different to viral marketing where the communication spreads. Word of mouse is similar but is transmitted via an internet-based platform.

The sharpest minds need the finest advice. **Kogan Page** creates success.

www.koganpage.com